150 Years of Song

HYMNODY IN THE REORGANIZATION, 1860–2010

by Richard Clothier

Herald Publishing House

Independence, Missouri

ISBN 978-0-830-91491-3

Cover and interior design and typesetting by John Hamer
Cover photos by Val Brinkerhoff, courtesy Community of Christ
Copy-editing by Michael Karpowicz

PRINTED IN THE UNITED STATES OF AMERICA

Table of Contents

Since Love is Lord of heaven and earth,
How can I keep from singing?

Robert Lowry, *Hymns of the Saints,* number 157

I. Prelude: The Gift of Song

Roy Cheville once wrote that "when something significant happens in a dynamic society, the people sing of it."[1] On April 6, 1860, something significant happened in Amboy, Illinois, and the people sang with gratitude. Today, 150 years later, we are still singing.

We are singing in celebration, because the year 2010 denotes a significant anniversary for Community of Christ (formerly the Reorganized Church of Jesus Christ of Latter Day Saints). It marks 150 years since Joseph Smith III took on his father's mantle as president and prophet of the "new organization" of the church. As with all anniversaries, it offers a good time to think about where we have been and where we are going. It presents a good opportunity for exploring the movement's heritage, with the hope that it will point the way to an enhanced future.

One of the best ways to truly understand our heritage is to not only study the events that happened, but to also try to discover what the people *felt* about what was happening. And, an important path to understanding the beliefs, hopes, and desires of a people can be found in studying the hymns that emerged in their worship, and the thoughts and passions expressed in these songs.

For as long as anyone knows, singing has been a natural part of worship, because this art, so natural and yet so complex, has the ability to communicate human emotions in a particular and peculiar way. We sing because we have discovered that through music, especially music paired with insightful poetry, we are able to impart the deepest of expressions and receive the most penetrating of revelations.

Exploring this phenomenon more deeply, it becomes obvious that the art of music has always been closely associated with words. When we sing, we are really engaging in a unique combination of two arts. Music alone, without words, has the ability to affect our deepest emotions, those that cannot be put into words. When this pure music is combined with verbal expression, another level is reached. Here the more specific expressions of words are combined with the more abstract spiritual expressions of music, and a dual art form results that can enhance, intensify, and illuminate a text, and minister to the very soul. Thus, instead of just saying "I love you," it can be much more effective and moving to sing it. That is why humankind has turned to music when there is no other way to share the depths yearning to be expressed. When that love is too deep for words, that longing too intense, that sorrow beyond description, or that joy unspeakable, there is music. For that reason, music can rightfully be called "the language of the spirit."

Because the musical art can both *express* and *reveal* truths of the spirit, music has, down through all of history, been closely teamed with religion, the ultimate expression of the yearnings of the human spirit. Both music and religion address not the tangible, but the spiritual side of human beings. There may be no practical purpose for beauty, nor for that matter, for faith. But whenever humankind has felt the need to communicate the most sacred expressions of the soul, some sort of music has been created. From primitive civilizations to those of the present day, this unique art has risen to its highest purpose at such times. In fact, through more than three thousand years of Hebrew and Christian history, music has been a part of Divine worship, and the Bible contains some of our earliest examples of worship through song.

In Old Testament times, music was expected to assist in bringing about a spiritual experience with Divinity. Second Kings 3:14–16 (NRSV) records:

> Elisha said . . . "But get me a musician." And then, while the musician was playing, the power of the Lord came on him. And he said, "Thus says the Lord . . ."

Martin Luther also had a deep appreciation for the art of music. He is quoted as saying, in 1538:

> After the Word of God, only music deserves to be praised as the mistress and governess of the emotions of the human heart . . . It is out of consideration for this power of music that the Fathers and Prophets willed, and not in vain, that nothing be more closely bound up with the Word of God than music.[2]

Hymns can give us valuable insights into the theology of a people of faith, and they can show us how the beliefs of a movement can evolve and change through time. As an example, one of the central tenets of Latter Day Saintism has been the concept of Zion. A brief examination of hymns on this subject will show how that concept has evolved through the years. In the earliest years of the movement, several variations of beliefs about Zion can be seen, including: (1) Zion as the city of God or Enoch's perfect city; (2) Zion as a place of refuge or safety; and (3) Zion as the "gathering" in Independence, Missouri.

These beliefs about Zion can all be found in hymns published in the movement's first hymnal, compiled by Emma Smith in 1835. The first of these is illustrated in the hymn "Glorious Things of Thee Are Spoken" (p. 11 in this volume), in lines such as "Zion, city of our God," and "On the Rock of Enoch founded." The second understanding is shown in the hymn "Guide Us, O Thou Great Jehovah" (not included in this volume), with phrases such as "Keep us safe on Zion's hill," and "Guard us in this holy home." The third concept is expressed in another hymn, W. W. Phelps's "There Is a Land the Lord Will Bless" (p. 13). In this hymn, Phelps identifies the place where "Israel gathers home" as Independence, Missouri (the "fields along Missouri's flood"). The important concept of gathering to Zion is clearly expressed in a number of hymns, including a revision of a popular song of the period, changed to read "Shall We Gather Home to Zion" (p. 46).

In 1909, the Reorganized Church received new instruction on the concept of Zion through Joseph Smith III. Section 128 of the Doctrine and Covenants affirms that Zion has no single geographic location and that Saints are called to live in interdependence with non-members in their communities. Thus, concepts such as that of Zion as an ensign to the world are found in hymns like "Send Forth Thy Light, O Zion!" (p. 90). And the more recent concept of Zion as a divine cause for which to labor, rather than as a finite goal to be completed, is reflected in the hymn, "The Cause of Zion Summons Us" (p. 95). These are only a few examples of the evolving theology of a people of faith, as expressed in their hymnody through the years.

Emma Smith (1804–1879)

The Latter Day Saint movement began with the conscientious searching of a young man for a right relationship with his God. From that experience evolved a unique religious faith that, in many variations, is now embraced by millions of people around the world. And, from the beginning, singing has played a central role in both expressing and shaping the faith of the people.

The narrative that follows traces the story of hymnody in Community of Christ through its nine hymnals.[3] It seems an opportune time for such an exploration, as the tenth hymnal in the sequence is currently in the planning process for a 2013 debut. The several examples cited from each of the hymnals are not meant to imply any judgment as to quality or importance, but are included only as illustrations of the song of each period. Any number of hymns might have served just as well. For the sake of historical interest, preference has been given whenever possible to illustrative hymns no longer found in *Hymns of the Saints*, the current hymnal of the church, which is readily available. In studying the examples, the reader will discern factors, both musical and theological, which limit the relevance of some of these hymns to worship in today's church.

One additional note should be added: portions of the narrative that follows have been previously published by the author in *Restoration Studies IX* (Independence: Herald Publishing House, 2005), and in the book *A Heritage of Hymns* (Independence: Herald Publishing House, 1996), neither of which is currently in print.

The visions and blessings of old are returning;
The angels are coming to visit the earth.
W. W. Phelps, "The Spirit of God Like a Fire Is Burning"*

II. The Story Begins

THE STORY OF HYMNODY in the Reorganization of the church founded by Joseph Smith Jr. necessarily begins with the birth of the Latter Day Saint movement itself. In fact, Latter Day Saints of all persuasions who enjoy singing can be thankful that the families of the founder and his wife, Emma Hale Smith, associated themselves with the Presbyterian and Methodist faith traditions, rather than with groups such as the Society of Friends that were also active in upstate New York at the time. For, while the Quakers had little use for music, the Methodists and Presbyterians enjoyed a rich tradition of singing. No doubt this background was of some influence when, three months after the April 6, 1830, organization of the church, the young prophet Joseph directed Emma, a capable singer, to compile the first hymnal of the church, in a revelation that ended with these now well-known words: "my soul delighteth in the song of the heart; yea, the song of the righteous is a prayer unto me."[4]

Emma accepted this responsibility, but the work did not progress rapidly. In addition to her normal duties, during the next 5½ years Emma was to experience three pregnancies, the adoption of twins, and three infant deaths.[5] In the meantime, a recent convert who had had some experience in journalism was charged with the responsibility of traveling from Kirtland to Independence in order to set up a printing press in the newly designated place for Zion. One of the tasks William Wines Phelps was asked to undertake was to "correct" the hymns Emma had

* The final hymn in the 1835 hymnal, and number 33 in *Hymns of the Saints*.

been selecting (revising them freely to ensure compatibility with Latter Day Saint doctrine) and begin printing them in the forthcoming church periodical, *The Evening and the Morning Star*.[6] When Emma's hymnal, dated 1835, finally came off the press not long before the dedication of the Kirtland temple in March 1836, the pocket-size volume contained ninety hymns texts. It included no music, and even though the names of the authors were also absent, about forty of the texts can be identified as having Latter Day Saint authors, the majority of them attributed to Phelps himself.[7]

Before long, it became apparent that more hymns were needed beyond the ninety that Emma had presented in her first hymnal, and that the thousand or so copies of the original hymnal printed in Kirtland were insufficient.[8] In 1839, the high priests assembled in Nauvoo voted that Emma should be the one designated to compile a second hymnal. Responding to this request, in 1841 she published her Nauvoo hymnal, a work that contained 304 hymns, including seventy-eight of the ninety from her Kirtland hymnal.

In the meantime, the dearth of hymnals was also being felt in the British mission, and it was decided there that three members of the Twelve who were laboring in that country, Parley P. Pratt, John Taylor, and Brigham Young, would compile a hymnal for the Saints in Europe. In 1840 the three apostles produced their hymnal in Manchester, England, with a first run of three thousand copies. Just as W. W. Phelps was a pivotal force and substantial contributor to the 1835 Kirtland hymnal, so Parley Pratt was to the 1840 Manchester hymnal, with no fewer than forty-seven of the 277 hymn texts being his. It appears that Joseph would have preferred that the missionaries wait for the publication of Emma's Nauvoo hymnal, which he considered would become the "standard work" for the church. However their collection seems to have gained his approval after the fact.[9]

Emma Smith did not end her work of compiling hymnals in 1841, but in fact went on to publish two more collections: her hymnal for the Reorganization, published in 1861, and an expanded version of the same book in 1864. These two works form the foundation for the body of hymnody represented in the seven major hymnals published since that time by the Reorganized Church of Jesus Christ of Latter Day Saints, now Community of Christ. A brief survey of these volumes will show them to be notable for the range of styles and content they encompass, reflective of the evolving cultural and theological milieu of their times. It is interesting to note that, while Emma's Nauvoo work became the basis for the hymnals of the Reorganization, the apostles' Manchester hymnal, which has been characterized by Michael Hicks as "better-suited to the expanding theology of Joseph's last years,"[10] is the work from which the hymnals of the Utah-based church flow.

Hymns of the Early Church, 1832–1836

Redeemer of Israel

When the first edition of *The Evening and the Morning Star* rolled off the press in Independence, Missouri, in June 1832, it included on the last page six hymn texts—one by Parley P. Pratt, two by the publisher, W. W. Phelps, and three by non–Latter Day Saints, all of them revised by Phelps. One of these hymns in particular has become one of the best-loved songs of the church. Phelps's robust hymn, "Redeemer of Israel," likened the trials of the early Saints to the tribulation of the children of Israel, and affirmed that "the kingdom is ours, and the hour of redemption is near." In writing this hymn, Phelps was strongly indebted to a text by the English hymn writer, Joseph Swain, published in London in 1791. Swain's hymn "O Thou in Whose Presence My Soul Takes Delight" first appeared in America in 1813, using the tune "Davis," the tune still used today for "Redeemer of Israel." "O Thou in Whose Presence" is reproduced on the following page exactly as it appeared in the 1820 song book *The Missouri Harmony*.

Notice that the music for this hymn is printed in what is known as "shape-note notation." This system was an early attempt to help people learn to read music, by printing the various notes of the musical scale in different shapes. As you look at it more closely, you will discover that the melody appears in the middle of the three staves, as was the custom at the time. Swain's text is a love song apparently addressed to God in

DAVIS. 11 and 8. 35

2 Where dost thou at noon-tide resort with thy sheep,
To feed on the pasture of love;
For why in the valley of death should I weep,
Alone in the wilderness rove.

3 O why should I wander an alien from thee,
Or cry in the desert for bread?
My foes would rejoice when my sorrows they see,
And smile at the tears I have shed.

4 Ye daughters of Zion, declare have you seen
The star that on Israel shone;
Say if in your tents my beloved hath been,
And where with his flock he hath gone.

5 This is my beloved, his form is divine,
His vestments shed odours around;
The locks on his head are as grapes on the vine,
When autumn with plenty is crown'd;

6 The roses of Sharon, the lillies that grow
In vales on the banks of the streams;
His cheeks in the beauty of excellence blow,
His eye all invitingly beams.

7 His voice, as the sound of a dulcimer sweet,
Is heard through the shadow of death,
The cedars of Lebanon bow at his feet,
The air is perfumed with his breath.

8 His lips as a fountain of righteousness flow,
That waters the garden of grace,
From which their salvation the gentiles shall know,
And bask in the smiles of his face.

9 Love sits on his eyelids and scatters delight,
Through all the bright mansions on high;
Their faces the cherubim veil in his sight,
And tremble with fulness of joy.

10 He looks, and ten thousands of angels rejoice,
And myriads wait for his word,
He speaks, and eternity, fill'd with his voice,
Re-echo's the praise of her Lord.

"O Thou in Whose Presence" as it appeared in the 1820 Missouri Harmony

12 SACRED HYMNS

And every man in every place,
Shall meet a brother and a friend.

HYMN 6. P. M.

1 Redeemer of Israel,
Our only delight,
On whom for a blessing we call;
Our shadow by day,
And our pillar by night,
Our king, our companion, our all.

2 We know he is coming
To gather his sheep,
And plant them in Zion, in love,
For why in the valley
Of death should they weep,
Or alone in the wilderness rove?

3 How long we have wander'd
As strangers in sin,
And cried in the desert for thee!
Our foes have rejoic'd
When our sorrows they've seen;
But Israel will shortly be free.

4 As children of Zion
Good tidings for us:
The tokens already appear;

SACRED HYMNS. 13

Fear not and be just,
For the kingdom is ours,
And the hour of redemption is near.

5 The secret of heaven,
The myst'ry below,
That many have sought for so long,
We know that we know,
For the Spirit of Christ,
Tells his servants they cannot be wrong.

HYMN 7. S. M.

1 See all creation join
To praise the eternal God;
The heavenly hosts begin the song,
And sound his name abroad.

2 The sun with golden beams,
And moon with silver rays;
The starry lights, and twinkling flames;
Shine to their Maker's praise.

3 He built those worlds above,
And fix'd their wondrous frame;
By his command they stand or move,
And always speak his name.

4 The fleecy clouds that rise,
Or falling showers or snow;

"Redeemer of Israel" as it appeared in Emma Smith's first hymnal (1835)

Jesus Christ, and was originally entitled "A Description of Christ by His Graces and Power." It is apparent that, in writing "Redeemer of Israel," Phelps borrowed and revised much of the material of the first three stanzas of Swain's poem, which are based on the Twenty-third Psalm, and little from the rest of the text, which is a paraphrase of portions of the Song of Solomon.

Phelps's text, like the two examples that follow, was included in Emma's first hymnal. The two-page spread on which the text was printed in that 1835 collection is reproduced above. Note that the fifth stanza is no longer sung, for reasons that should be obvious.

Glorious Things of Thee Are Spoken

THIS HYMN IS another that was published in the first edition of *The Evening and the Morning Star* in 1832. It is a hymn that was not written by a Latter Day Saint, but it concerned one of the movement's most important concepts—Zion. And, particularly after Phelps's "fine-tuning" of the text, it was one that spoke deeply to the hearts of the early Saints. In fact, the minutes of the first three church conferences to name the hymns that were sung all mention this same hymn.

Written by the Englishman John Newton, who also authored "Amazing Grace," the text is based on ideas from Isaiah and the Psalms. Among Phelps's alterations were changing "formed thee" to "chose thee" and "rock of ages" to "rock of Enoch" in stanza one, and changing "eternal love" to "celestial love" in stanza two. In stanza three, Phelps changed "Safe they feed upon the manna" to "Sweetly they enjoy the Spirit." Stanza four revisions included altering "their hopes rely on" to "their souls rely on" and changing "Over self to reign as King" to the more theologically interesting phrase, "With himself to reign as kings."

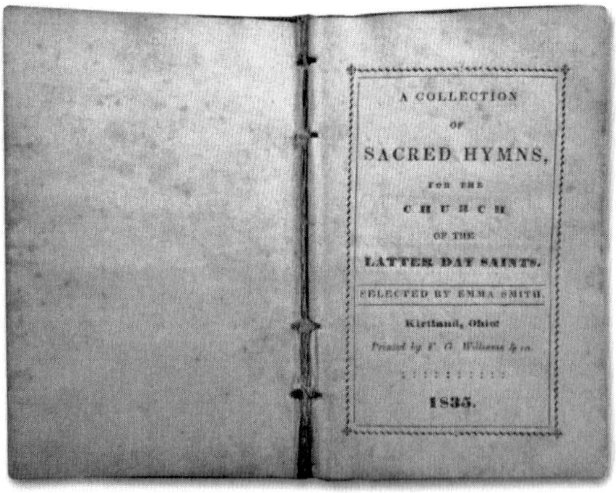

Emma Smith's 1835 hymnal

Perhaps partly because of Phelps's revisions, Newton's hymn resonated deeply with the early Saints as they pursued their quest for a community of which "glorious things" would be spoken—"Zion, city of our God." The full text of this hymn, as printed in Emma's first hymnal, comprised ten stanzas. The first eight are included here as four double stanzas. The tune "Austria," most often associated with the hymn, was written by the great eighteenth-century classical composer Franz Joseph Haydn for the birthday of the Austrian Emperor Francis II.

Glorious Things of Thee are Spoken

John Newton (1725-1807), rev. W. W. Phelps (1792-1872) Franz Joseph Haydn (1732-1809)

There Is a Land the Lord Will Bless

A PARTICULARLY INTERESTING HYMN text appeared in the September 1834 issue of *The Evening and the Morning Star*. By that time, Phelps's printing press in Independence had been destroyed by an angry mob and the Saints who were gathering there driven out. The periodical was now being printed in Kirtland with Oliver Cowdery as editor, but the hymn is nevertheless the work of W. W. Phelps. The verses were included in a letter from Phelps to Cowdery that expressed with great emotion the severe conditions of persecution the Saints were facing at the time. In this poem which ends his letter, Phelps looks forward to the day when persecution will cease and Zion will at last be established, and also reminds us where that gathering is to be.

In his longing for the imminent return of Zion, Phelps clearly identifies, in stanza three, the location to which the "pure in heart [will] return" as being "the fields along Missouri's flood," the modern-day river that Phelps likens to the Biblical river of Jordan. The Missouri was to be the river that latter-day Israel would cross to reach the Promised Land. After being violently driven out only a year earlier, W. W. Phelps had not given up on Independence, Missouri, as the place for Zion. But he had a harsh end in mind for those who had so violently opposed the Saints. For he wrote, "Before the word goes forth—'Destroy!' and all the wicked burn, with songs of everlasting joy the pure in heart return."

As was often the case, Phelps's verses were inspired by an existing hymn, this time a text of Isaac Watts, which begins, "There is a land of pure delight." But once again, Phelps infuses the text with distinctive Latter Day Saint passion to create a powerful hymn for his time. The hymn was included in Emma's first hymnal for the church, but was dropped in future hymnals as the concept of Zion broadened. For this volume we have abridged the hymn from eight stanzas to four, and have set it to a spirited tune of the day known as "Pisgah," found in both the *Kentucky Harmony* of 1817 and the *Southern Harmony* of 1847. (Remember that the early hymnals contained only texts, and in most cases we have no idea what tunes were used. In fact, different tunes were probably used in different locations, according to what melodies were known in a particular area.)

There Is A Land The Lord Will Bless

W. W. Phelps (1792-1872) | Scottish melody arr. J.C.Lowry, 1817. PISGAH

The Spirit of God Like a Fire Is Burning

THE WEEKS LEADING UP to the completion and dedication of the Kirtland Temple in March 1836 were filled with experiences that could only be described as Pentecostal in nature. Tongues, visions, and prophecies were enjoyed on several occasions. In one particular quorum session, those attending reported "a great flow of the Holy Spirit . . .like fire in their bones, so that they could not hold their peace, but were constrained to cry hosanna to God and the Lamb."[11]

With his poetic gifts, W. W. Phelps formulated the words of a hymn that caught up the powerful spirit of this remarkable period. Immediately after its publication in *The Messenger and Advocate,* the new hymn was printed as the last entry in Emma's hymnal, which actually came off the presses only a few weeks before the Temple dedication. It has long since secured a place in the hearts of Latter Day Saints of all persuasions.

Set to a stirring English tune, this hymn was sung at the dedication of the Kirtland Temple by a large choir situated in the special choir pews at all four corners of the Temple. It was surely a most moving and memorable moment, for it is recorded that the benedictory prayer by Sidney Rigdon was "ended with loud acclamations of Hosanna! Hosanna! Hosanna to God and the Lamb, Amen, Amen, and Amen."[12]

In 1844, a small unofficial hymnal was published in Bellows Falls, Vermont, by J. C. Little and G. B. Gardner. This book is notable in that it included, for the first time, a soprano and bass line of musical notation for thirty-one out of the total of forty-eight hymns. "The Spirit of God Like a Fire Is Burning" was the first entry in this booklet, and it is reproduced here exactly as it appeared in 1844. It would be forty-five years until music would be included in an official Latter Day Saint hymnal. Notice that the tune is the one still used today, but that Phelps's original hymn consisted of six stanzas.

"The Spirit of God Like a Fire Is Burning" as it appeared in the 1844 Little and Gardner hymnal
(*The text is continued on the following page*)

6 SACRED

5 Old Israel that fled from the world for his freedom,
Must come with the cloud and the pillar amain.
A Moses, and Aaron, and Joshua lead him,
And feed him on manna from heaven again.
We'll sing and we'll shout, &c.

6 How blessed the day when the lamb and the lion
Shall lie down together without any ire;
And Ephraim be crown'd with his blessings in Zion,
As Jesus descends with his chariots of fire!
We'll sing and we'll shout with HIS armies, &c.

William Wines Phelps (1792–1872)

But Saints who know his endless love
Should sing his praises best.

"See All Creation Join," W. W. Phelps*

III. A Hymnal for the Reorganization

AFTER THE MIGRATION to Utah, while the Salt Lake Valley was blossoming with its multitudes, efforts were being made back in the Midwest to "gather the remnants." Even before the "new organization of the church"[13] was formally effected in Amboy, Illinois, on April 6, 1860, those who had been working toward organizing with "young Joseph" (Joseph Smith III) as prophet showed a desire to continue their rich tradition of singing. In his *Memoirs,* W. W. Blair records that a conference held in Amboy in June 1859 took action to provide for the publication of a hymnal "based upon the hymns published in a former edition, selected and compiled by Sister Emma, the wife of Joseph the Seer."[14]

Only a few months after the April 1860 organizational meeting, a conference that convened in Sandwich, Illinois, in October confirmed this action by voting that "Sister Emma Smith Bidaman [sic] be appointed to make a selection of hymns, to make a hymn-book," and that "Bro. Isaac Sheen be authorized to publish the said hymn-book on the most advantageous terms."[15] The same resolution instructed the branch presidents "to obtain subscriptions for the hymn-book and forward the same to Bro. Israel L. Rogers, the Bishop of the Church, or to Bro. Isaac Sheen."[16] In reporting the action of the conference, the October issue of *The True Latter Day Saints' Herald* spelled out the obvious rationale for Emma's selection: "Sister Emma Smith Bidaman [sic] was appointed by a revelation in July, 1830, to make a collection of sacred hymns . . .

*Adapted from Isaac Watts. Page 13 in Emma Smith's 1835 hymnal, and number 7 in her 1861 hymnal for the Reorganization.

She has therefore been re-appointed to the performance of this work."[17] The editor goes on to ask those who may wish to contribute hymns to forward them to Emma at Nauvoo, and adds the plea, "If they are written, they must be plain and legible."[18] The price of the books was set at fifty cents each. Thus began a series of publications by the Reorganized church which, in its efforts to enhance the musical life of the body, would encompass a rather remarkable degree of variety.

Emma's collection, called simply *The Latter Day Saints' Selection of Hymns*, was published (by "The Church of Jesus Christ of Latter Day Saints") in Cincinnati in 1861 and was, as suggested by the action of the 1859 conference, patterned closely after her Nauvoo hymnal of 1841. In fact, all but ten of the 249 hymns were common to that previous collection of 304 hymns, among them seventy of the ninety hymns she had selected for her Kirtland hymnal, and fifty-eight that had first been printed in the Manchester collection. In 1864, an enlarged edition was published, adding thirty-seven texts, including seven by David Hyrum Smith, the youngest son of Emma and the martyr, born less than five months after his father's assassination.

It is significant that the Reorganization began with a hymnal that was essentially a revision of Emma's Nauvoo work, rather than with the Manchester collection. This fact is noteworthy not only because Emma identified herself with the Reorganization while the apostles who had compiled the Manchester work went West, but also, as Michael Hicks and others have pointed out, because the 1841 Nauvoo compilation appears to be more in harmony with the hymnody of mainstream Christianity than was the 1840 Manchester collection embraced by the Utah church.[19] Since it may be said that the theology of a body is not only *expressed* but to some degree *shaped* by the hymns it sings, this factor, in addition to being significant at the time, may well have helped set the courses traveled since then by the two organizations.

Among the examples cited by Hicks of this "shift in emphasis" in Emma's Nauvoo hymnal, to be carried over to the Reorganization, are Newton's "Amazing Grace," and Watts's "When I Survey the Wondrous Cross," both of which appear in the Nauvoo hymnal but not in the Manchester collection.[20] It should be noted also that these two hymns are included in the current Community of Christ hymnal, but not the present LDS hymnbook. Additionally, distinctive texts from subsequent editions of the Manchester hymnal, such as "Praise to the Man Who Communed with Jehovah," and "The Glorious Gospel Light Has Shone," with its theme of baptism for the dead, are still to be found in the current LDS hymnal. The latter hymn has never appeared in Reorganization hymnals; but "Praise to the Man" was added in an appendix in the 1864 edition of Emma's Reorganization hymnal, and it appeared in the 1870 and 1889 RLDS hymnals in an altered form that began, "Praise to the Lord for the great restoration."

A glimpse of the challenges faced by the young church may be seen in notices that appeared from time to time in issues of the *Herald*. In the December 1860 issue, the editors expressed their frustration with "the extreme backwardness in forwarding subscriptions for the Hymn Book,"[21] and began publishing in each issue the names of those who had sent in their subscriptions. Only thirteen names appeared in that issue. In the fifth issue of the following year, which did not appear until August, the editors explained,

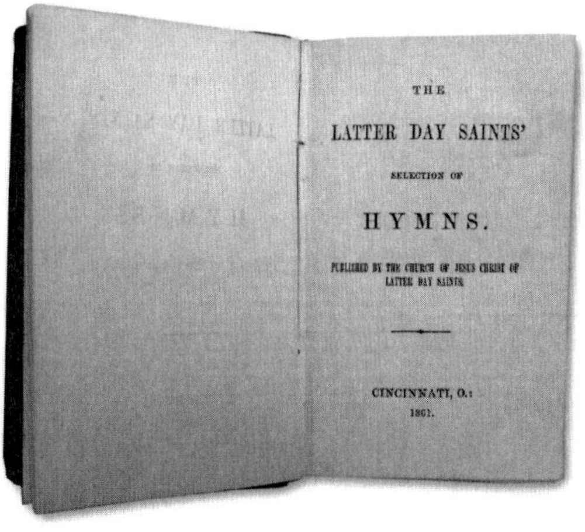

Emma Smith's 1861 hymnal for the Reorganization

> The delay of the ***Herald*** is caused by the inadequate supply of funds for the publication of it and the Hymn Book combined. If we could sell the hymn books which we have on hand, and if our numerous ***delinquent*** subscribers to the ***Herald*** would pay their subscriptions, our embarrassment would cease. . . If we cannot publish [the ***Herald***] ***regularly*** we can publish it ***irregularly***.[22]

The following three examples from the 1861 hymnal will serve to illustrate the variety of hymns in that collection.

Hymns from the First Reorganization Hymnal, 1861

See All Creation Join

Emma Smith included this text in all of her hymnals, including her two hymnals for the Reorganization. It was retained in the hymnals of 1870 and 1889, but has been largely forgotten since. "See All Creation Join" is a beautiful hymn of praise to God in nature, adapted from verses written by the great English hymn writer Isaac Watts (1674–1748), a man often referred to as "the father of English hymnody." Watts wrote more than six hundred hymns, most of them lyrical paraphrases of the Psalms. With their elegant and powerful simplicity, these hymns departed from the long tradition of English psalm-singing and ushered in what has been called the "golden age" of English hymnody. Perhaps if it were not for Watts, we would still be singing repetitious psalm chants, instead of the beautiful, meaningful hymns we love today.

Watts actually wrote no fewer than sixteen stanzas for this particular hymn, which originally began, "*Let every creature* join to praise the eternal God." For the church's first hymnal, W. W. Phelps revised Watts's text to create a hymn of praise containing five stanzas and a repeated refrain. The refrain, adapted from Watts's last stanza, conveys the meaningful challenge that "Saints who know His endless love, should sing His praises best."

For this volume, we have set this text to the tune "Terra Beata," often used for another hymn with a similar message of God in nature, "This Is My Father's World."

See All Creation Join

Isaac Watts (1674-1748), revised, W. W. Phelps

TERRA BEATA

Traditional English Melody, adapted by Franklin Sheppard (1852-1930)

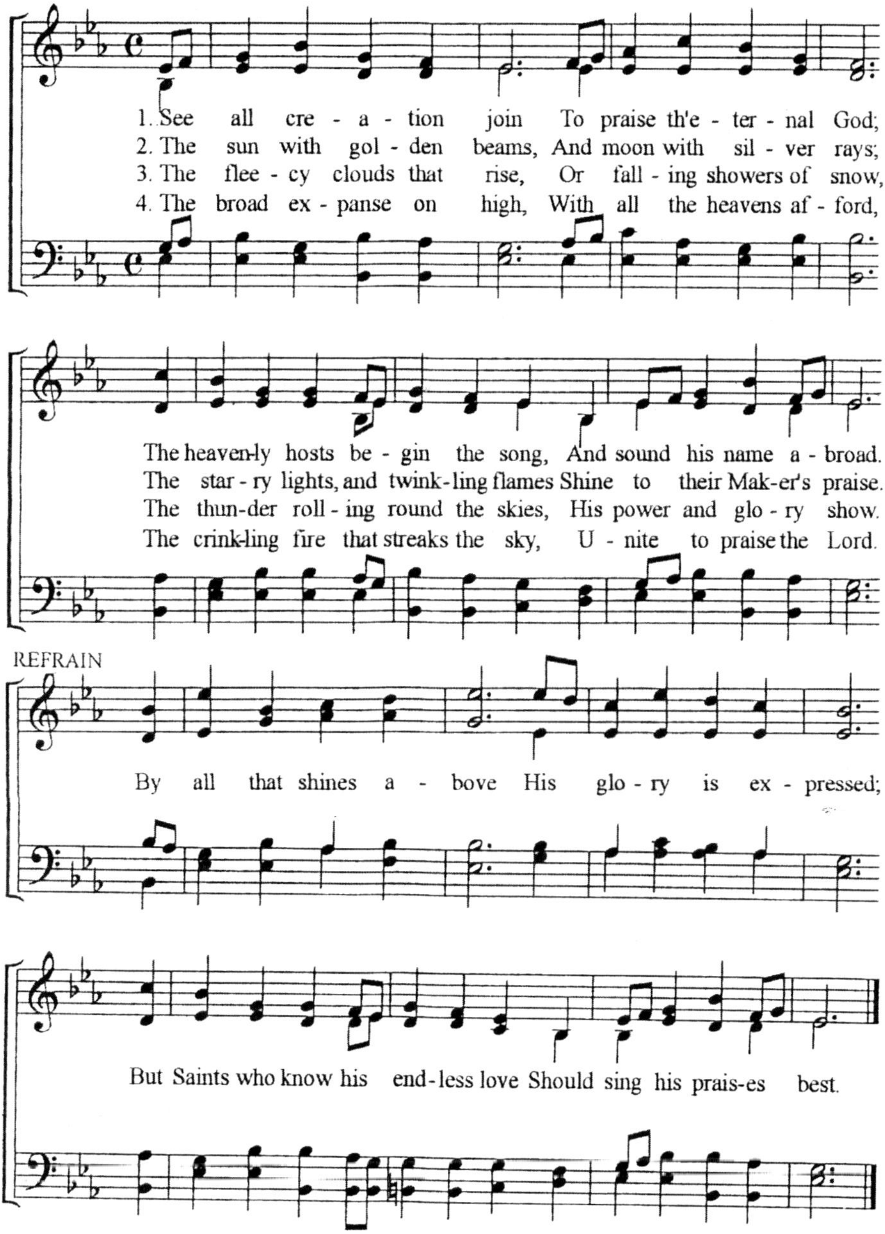

Phelps's adaptation of Isaac Watts's hymn "Let Every Creature Join to Praise"
(Phelps's third stanza is omitted here)

The Morning Breaks, the Shadows Flee

THIS HYMN, written by Parley P. Pratt, appeared in the 1840 Manchester hymnal, the collection compiled by Pratt and the other two apostles serving in England at the time. Like his fellow poet, W. W. Phelps, Pratt had been converted to the movement after reading the Book of Mormon and went on to become one of the pioneers of the Restoration movement. Pratt's influence in the growth of the early church was especially pivotal, because it was he who converted his friend in Ohio, Sidney Rigdon, to the young Latter Day Saint movement. Rigdon in turn converted many of his Disciples of Christ followers, thus beginning the highly important work in the Kirtland area.

Kirtland Temple

The strong expression of Parley Pratt's secure and confident faith in the imminent coming of the Kingdom of Heaven is proclaimed in this hymn, which secured pride of place as the first hymn in the Manchester collection. Pratt, like many of the early hymn writers, speaks of the ultimate triumph of "truth" over "error," which truth will soon burst forth "o'er the nations." Like W. W. Phelps, Pratt again likens the Saints, as "Judah's remnant," to ancient Israel, who soon "shall in their promised Canaan stand."

The hymn is reproduced here set to "Duke Street," from the 1933 *Saints' Hymnal*. This well-known tune is attributed to an eighteenth-century Englishman, John Hatton, about whom little is known, except that he apparently once lived on a street called "Duke Street" in Windle, Lancashire, England.

411

DUKE STREET. L. M.

P. P. Pratt, in 1841 Emma Smith Edition John Hatton, (?)–1793

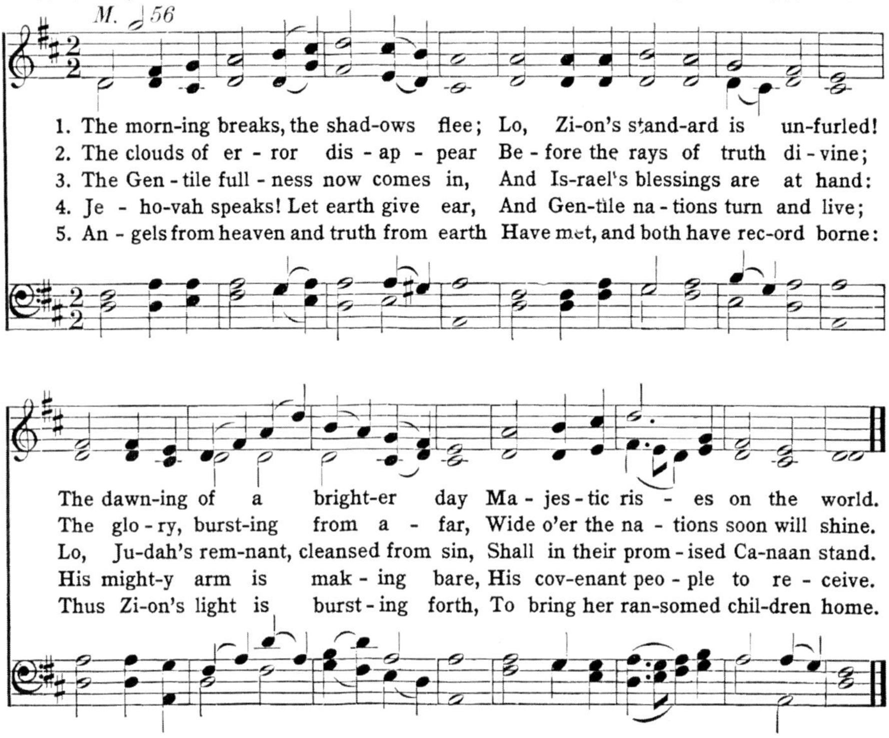

Parley P. Pratt (1807–1857)

When I Survey the Wondrous Cross

One of hymns cited as illustrating the broader outlook of Emma's Nauvoo and Reorganization hymnals is another hymn by Isaac Watts, "When I Survey the Wondrous Cross." It is a text that is today regarded as one of the finest hymns in the English language. Written in 1707 as a communion hymn, it is based on Galatians 6:14: "God forbid that I should glory, save in the cross of our Lord Jesus Christ, by whom the world is crucified unto me, and I unto the world."

This is a hymn that beautifully expresses a deeply felt understanding of the significance of Christ's crucifixion: "See from his head, his hands, his feet, sorrow and love flow mingled down!" It ends with this intimate response to the sacrifice of the Master: "Love so amazing, so divine, demands my soul, my life, my all." This text is said to be one of the earliest English hymns to use the pronoun "I" to express the deeply personal experience of the Christian faith.

Isaac Watts (1674–1748)

The language of Watts's hymns has the appeal of eloquent simplicity. Most of his texts are composed of one and two-syllable words that are easy to sing and to remember, yet profound in their meaning, for example, "O God, Our Help in Ages Past," and "Joy to the World! The Lord is Come."

For historic purposes, this text of Watts's has been set here to the tune "Effingham," with which it was paired in the 1889 *Saints' Harmony*. This tune, based on a folk melody, was first published in 1832 in the Mennonite shape-note hymnal *Harmonia Sacra*.

When I Survey the Wondrous Cross

Isaac Watts (1674-1748)

Anon., in *Prayer Meeting Tune Book*, Philadelphia, 1859
EFFINGHAM (as found in 1889 *Saints' Harmony*)

*A miscellany of early hymnals from the Community of Christ Archives —
Top row (left to right): the 1835 hymnal, the 1841 hymnal, the 1861 hymnal, the 1864 hymnal, and the 1870* Saints' Harp;
Bottom row (left to right): the 1889 Saints' Harmony, *a 1928 printing of the 1895* Saints' Hymnal, *and the 1903* Zion's Praises

I love, but ah, the sweet refrain,
"On Thee, my Savior, I depend."
*Joseph Smith III, "Unmoved by Fear"**

IV. *The Saints' Harp, 1870*

OUR STORY MOVES on to New Year's Day 1865, when a significant baptism into the Reorganized Church took place in none other than Salt Lake City, Utah, as a talented individual named Mark H. Forscutt joined the Reorganization. Forscutt, a native of Godmanchester, England, had been converted to Mormonism in 1835 against the strong desires of his family, resulting in his leaving home. His total dedication to the movement caused him to give up a place at Cambridge University and take up a mission in his native land.

After serving several years as a missionary in England, Forscutt was persuaded to join "the gathering," and sailed with his new bride for America in March 1860. After pushing a handcart from Nebraska to Salt Lake City, this talented individual served for a time as private secretary to Brigham Young. He soon became disillusioned, partly, according to his daughter, because of the pressure he felt to practice plural marriage.[23] For a time he joined with the Morrisite movement in Utah and was ordained an apostle in that group.

After joining the Reorganization, Forscutt began to feel that his life was in danger as an "apostate," and he left Utah under the veil of secrecy, leaving his family to follow later. He made his way back to the Midwest, where he soon became a close friend of Joseph Smith III. A gifted orator, Forscutt would be the one selected by Joseph to preach the funeral sermon for his mother, Emma. His command of language, as well as his self-training in music, were to find expression in several positions of leadership and ministry and, notably, in the next two hymnals of the

* *The Saints' Harp*, number 10.

Joseph Smith III (1832–1914)

David H. Smith (1844–1904)

church. The account of the annual Conference in St. Louis on April 6, 1869, included the following action:

> The compilation of a new hymn book was authorized by resolution, and Joseph Smith appointed on the committee of compilation, he to choose his associates. He chose M. H. Forscutt and David H. Smith, and also appointed Norman W. Smith to act in case D. H. Smith was gone on his mission before the completion of the work.[24]

All four of the individuals named in this action were already active in writing or composing hymns. Joseph, like his brother David, was a published poet, and Norman W. Smith (no relation to the church's first family) had often been called upon by Joseph to write music for the texts he composed. But it was Mark Forscutt who would become the driving force in RLDS hymnody during the next two decades.

To say that the hymnal that resulted from the 1869 Conference action was ambitious would be an understatement. Forscutt had anticipated that he would be called upon to head up such a project, and had previously filled several notebooks with hymns, some of which he remembered from England, some from Utah, and some which he composed himself. Thus, by the next year, 1870, Forscutt and his committee had produced *The Saints' Harp*, a collection of no less than 1,120 hymn texts filling 792 4×6-inch pages. More than two-thirds of the texts in Emma's 1861 hymnal had been retained, and hundreds of texts from a variety of sources were added, including eighty-eight new texts by Forscutt himself, forty-nine by David H. Smith, and thirty-four by Joseph Smith III. In a lengthy preface, the committee anticipated concern over the size of the hymnal, and explained its rationale, addressing a dilemma faced by hymnal committees everywhere:

> The size of the book may be objected to by some; but we do not believe the objection will be persisted in when it is considered that the number of tastes we were required to select hymns to suit is so great, and of so varied a character, that but few if any hymns ever written would have suited all. Had we selected what only gratified us, some would have been ungratified; and had we selected only what would have pleased some of these whose choice would not be ours, others of them would still have been displeased.[25]

The committee went on to state that "a very respectable number of our brethren and sisters have desired that we should furnish tunes with this book of hymns . . ." It explained that this would have made the book too expensive for many members, and also cited the problem of differing musical tastes in the church, so that "while we might please many, we should not please all." Thus, it suggested that the church appoint a separate committee on music for a future hymnal.[26] This recommendation would soon be followed.

Included on the following pages are examples of hymns from the 1870 hymnal: a hymn by the prophet, Joseph III, and three by his younger brother, David H. Smith. The musical settings for each of these hymns are taken from later hymnals.

Hymns from *The Saints' Harp*, 1870

Unmoved by Fear, My Praise is Due

The prophet Joseph Smith III had a poetic inclination. As has been pointed out, both he and his younger brother, David Hyrum, contributed a significant number of hymn texts to the Reorganization, most of them appearing for the first time in Forscutt's *Saints' Harp*. Joseph wrote this text during the early years of his presidency, and it continues to be sung today. It expresses the deep faith of one who had found an intimately personal relationship with his God.

This hymn teaches us that true praise is not praise that is prompted by fear, but rather "taught" us by God's own all-encompassing love. Our only fear is that we will be found unworthy to walk beside our "noblest Friend." The prophet praises God for his mercy and counsel, and ends with the simple prayer of faith, "On thee, my Savior, I depend." These are the expressions of one who, in spite of doubts and perhaps even some fears, had reluctantly made the decision to accept the challenge of the prophetic role left by the death of his father. It is an affirmation of the faith of a leader who would shape the "new organization" of the church for years to come.

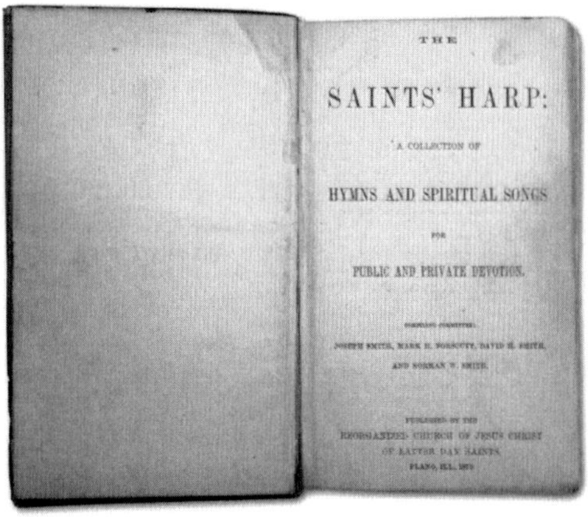

The Saints' Harp (*1870*)

This hymn is reproduced here as it appears in the 1933 *Saints' Hymnal*. It is set to the tune "Park Street," written in the early nineteenth century by a British musician with an impressive name, Frederick Marco Antonio Venua.

21

PARK STREET. L. M.

Joseph Smith, 1832-1914 Frederick M. A. Venua, 1810

"Unmoved by Fear" as it appeared in the 1933 Saints' Hymnal

Let Us Shake Off the Coals from Our Garments

David Hyrum Smith was the last son of Emma and Joseph Smith Jr., born less than five months after the martyrdom of his father in 1844. His formative years were spent in the stress and struggle of those unsettling times, and he found solace in his pursuits of music, art, and poetry. As he grew to adulthood he became active in the Reorganization, led by his older brother, Joseph III. Sadly, David began to show early signs of mental illness when he was only in his twenties, although he continued to function as an effective minister, including serving a mission to Utah. In 1873 he was called to the First Presidency. He was released from this responsibility in 1883, and his later years were spent in an institution, thus depriving the church of a brilliant and charismatic personality.

This particular hymn came out of a rather remarkable experience at a prayer meeting held during an 1863 church conference in Manti, in western Iowa. During the meeting, Joseph III rose and began to prophesy. He told the Saints that if they remained faithful, they would prosper and be blessed, but warned them to beware, lest division and tribulation sweep them away and "dash them upon the rocks of misfortune."

Immediately, young David arose and sang the first two stanzas of this song, which included several ideas from his brother's prophecy. It was a message of encouragement to the people, sung to a familiar folk tune of the day. It was a call for commitment, phrased in poetic imagery from the heart of a young man who grew to adulthood along the shores of a great river: "Let us anchor our barks in the center, and be safe from the rocks on the shore."

The hymn is reproduced here as it appears in the 1933 *Saints' Hymnal*.

Opposite: "Let Us Shake Off the Coals From Our Garments" as it appeared in the 1933 Saints' Hymnal

188

LET US SHAKE OFF THE COALS. 10. 9. 10. 9. D.

David H. Smith, 1844-1904 — Old Melody. Arranged by Editors

Let Us Pray for One Another

HERE IS ANOTHER of the beloved hymns of David H. Smith. As a young man, David was no doubt familiar with the often repeated request by the Saints to be remembered in prayer. He would have attended countless prayer services, beginning with those in private homes in Nauvoo with his brother Joseph presiding. It was in settings such as this that the admonition to pray for one another was most frequently heard, and it was on these occasions that this hymn was most often sung.

The 1981 *Hymns of the Saints* replaced David H. Smith's original text with a hymn by Maurice Draper that carries the same title, but is essentially a new hymn based on some of Smith's key phrases. Draper's hymn begins with the same first line, but endeavors to remain on a more positive level than the original text, in which the first two stanzas in particular contain rather dark imagery. In doing so, however, some of the intent of the original is lost, along with its unique window into the beliefs and thought processes of that time, beautifully expressed. The only other hymn in *Hymns of the Saints* traditionally attributed to David H. Smith, "You May Sing of the Beauty" (HS 8), has recently been discovered to actually be the work of one William Hunter, published in 1845 in *The Minstrel of Zion* (Philadelphia: Sorin and Ball). This means that, in actuality, no hymns by this eminent figure of the early Restoration continue in the church's repertoire today.

Although it was first included in the 1870 *Saints' Harp*, the hymn is reproduced here as it appeared in the 1933 *Saints' Hymnal*, set to a Scottish tune arranged for the 1889 *Saints' Harmony*, presumably by Mark Forscutt.

311 The Saintly Life

DECATUR. 8. 7. 8. 7. D.

David H. Smith, 1844–1904 — Revised from "Saints' Harmony," 1889

"Let Us Pray for One Another" reproduced from the 1933 Saints' Hymnal

Before the Morning's Joyous Light

David H. Smith was loved and admired by the people of the Reorganization, who often referred to him as "the sweet singer of Israel." As would be expected, his forty-nine hymn texts in *The Saints' Harp* abound in expressions and theology that were current in his day, but often seem outmoded to us now. One additional hymn from his pen, however, will be included here. It has not been published in any of our hymnals since 1889, and thus has probably never been sung since. Nevertheless, it gives us an appreciation for the young author's love of both nature and the gospel, and his linkage of these two driving forces in his life. The comparisons he makes between the brightness of the rising sun and the all-surpassing light of God illustrate the poetic and sensitive nature of this talented young man who served God with his all. His hymn for a new day ends appropriately with the familiar phrase from Psalm 30:5, "Joy cometh in the morn."

In the version printed here, the fourth stanza of the original text has been omitted and several textual revisions have been made in an attempt to update the language, with the intention that this might be a hymn that can find some usefulness today. The text has been set to the graceful English hymn tune "Repton." In order to remain faithful to the poet, David H. Smith's original text is also printed below:

Before the morning's joyous light
The shades of night retire;
Those lesser lamps that seemed so bright,
Awed by the sun's majestic might
In his broad beams expire.

So may truth's everlasting beam
Shine in each willing heart,
And error, that like night doth seem,
Fade like an uninstructive dream,
And evermore depart.

May this fair day be wisely spent
As given of the Lord;
Remember it is only lent,
Its hours like golden vases sent
With good works to be stored.

With skillful hands each task perform,
Our minds on truth intent,
Filled with good thoughts, like sunshine [warm,
That all the weariness shall charm,
Throughout this day's extent.

Oh! Guide us Father, on our way
To that eternal bourne;
Order our lives from day to day
Till we each dawn may gladly say,
'Joy cometh in the morn.'

Before the morning's joyous light

David H. Smith (1844-1904), revised R. C. C. Hubert H. Parry (1848-1918)

REPTON

A lovely hymn by David H. Smith, recently revised

Yes, we'll gather home to Zion,
Our beautiful, our beautiful Zion!
Gather with the saints home to Zion,
And be saved in the Kingdom of God.
T. W. Smith, *The Saints' Harmony*, number 963

V. *The Saints' Harmony, 1889*

THE SUGGESTION BY the *Saints' Harp* committee that a separate committee on music for a future hymnal be appointed was acted on in due course. At the September 1871 Conference, held near Council Bluffs, Iowa,

> A resolution was passed, on the 22nd, authorizing the appointment of a committee to collect matter for the Saints' Harp. The President appointed M. H. Forscutt, N. W. Smith, D. H. Smith, J. A. Scott, John T. Kinnaman, William Roberts, and Phineas Cadwell.[27]

By the collection of "matter" for *The Saints' Harp*, the resolution alluded to the addition of tunes for the 1,120 texts of that volume.

The work progressed slowly. Over the next seventeen years, numerous changes took place in the make-up of the committee, including the release of Forscutt for a time while he was on a mission to Europe, and even the release of the entire committee in 1876. In 1887, counsel given through Joseph III settled questions about music in the church by encouraging members to cultivate "the gifts of music and of song." The revelation stated, "The service of song in the house of the Lord with humility and unity of Spirit in them that sing and them that hear is blessed, and acceptable with God..." The document accepted the use of instruments "as wisdom and choice may direct," with the exception that instruments were to "be silent when the Saints assemble for prayer and testimony..." The same counsel urged the acceleration of the hymnal project with these words: "To facilitate unity in the song service of the church those to whom the work of providing a book of song has been intrusted [sic] may hasten their work in its time."[28]

The following year, Mark Forscutt was reappointed as the editor of the hymnal, and *The Saints' Harmony* was finally published in Lamoni, Iowa in 1889. It was a massive, unique work made up of split pages, with more than seven hundred tunes on the top half, and the 1,120 texts from *The Saints' Harp* on the bottom. The texts were numbered, but the tunes were not, being identified only by their name and the page on which the tune began. In order to find a suggested tune for a desired text, one had to flip through the top half of the book and search for a tune that had the number of that text printed above it. This process was aided by the fact that the tunes were printed more or less in the numerical order of the texts for which they were suggested, however in many cases several text numbers were printed above a given tune. Thus, while this novel approach may have slowed the process of matching texts and tunes, it may also have encouraged the use of alternate melodies.

No fewer than 127 of the tunes printed in *The Saints' Harmony* were written by Mark Forscutt himself, using his own name and nine pseudonyms.[29] Instead of a pocket-size volume, as previous hymnals had been, this monumental work measured 8½×11 inches, was 1½ inches thick, and weighed more than three pounds. In addition to the hymns, it included seven anthems, twenty-seven pages of indexes, and even a twelve-page short course in music theory.

An excerpt from the long preface to this work provides an insight into the sources of the tunes presented in the collection and, moreover, into the feeling of accomplishment Forscutt must have felt in publishing this ambitious project.

> We may surely be pardoned if we rejoice that in *The Saints' Harmony* about four hundred and fifty compositions are published for the first time to the world, that five hundred and two pieces are published for the first time in America, and that three hundred and ninety-three of these are original contributions by our own composers, written with the intention of their being first published in *The Saints' Harmony.*[30]

Mark Forscutt had produced a book that was by far the largest collection of hymnody in the history of all Latter Day Saintism. The reader cannot help but be amazed by the statement in another paragraph of the preface wherein he reveals that he had "contemplated a more extensive" work!

It will come as no surprise to modern readers that this most ambitious of all the church's hymnals was not well received. The book was large and cumbersome, and expensive for the time at $2.50 per copy. And, of course, most people could not read music, so it would seem unrealistic to expect that so many unfamiliar tunes could be effectively learned by the congregations. This was especially true in that many of the tunes were either newly composed or arranged, or of European origin. Perhaps the only surprise is that it was six years before action was taken to initiate a more modest and usable collection of hymns.

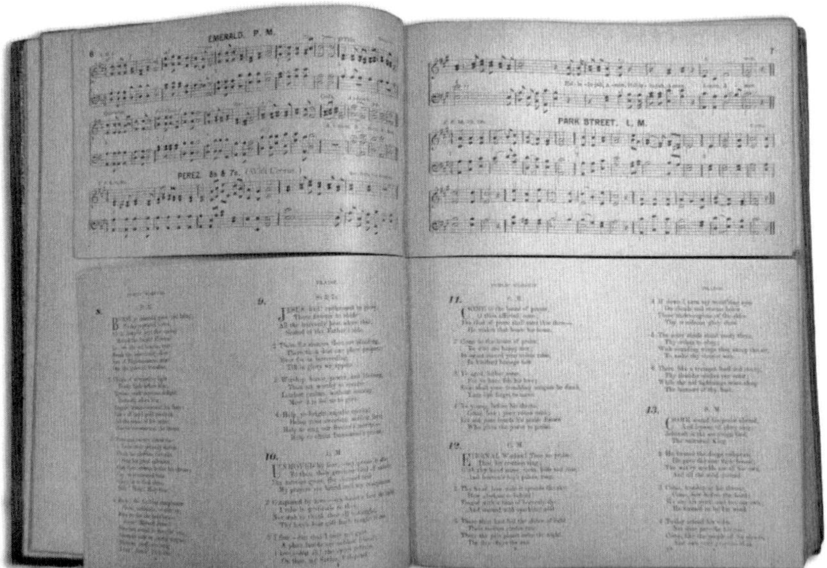

The split-page Saints' Harmony *(1889)*

Hymns from *The Saints' Harmony*, 1889

Burst, Ye Emerald Gates, and Bring

The importance of the leadership of Mark Forscutt in many areas, including missionary work, publishing, and music, has been pointed out. The 1889 *Saints' Harmony* was in many ways his crowning achievement. This enormous undertaking provided music for each of the 1,120 hymns in his earlier *Saints' Harp,* a good deal of it written by Forscutt himself. Two of his 88 hymn texts and two of his 127 hymn tunes are still being sung today. One of these tunes, "Emerald," is used twice in today's *Hymns of the Saints,* matched with the texts, "Every Good and Perfect Gift" (HS 151), and "Go Now Forth into the World" (HS 436).

"Emerald" was originally written by Forscutt to be used with a text found in the 1849 Adventist publication *The Advent Harp,* which begins, "Burst, ye emerald gates, and bring to my raptured vision." This strong, buoyant tune was written under the name "Hilliare," one of the several pseudonyms he used in this hymnal. One assumes that he did not want people to realize that the editor of the hymnal included so many of his own tunes in the collection.

This hymn is reproduced on the following two pages in its original format, that is, with the tune at the top (p. 42) and the text at the bottom (p. 43) of the split pages. Each half page was often shared with more than one text or tune. (Note that the text to "Unmoved By Fear" is on the same page.)

Forscutt's tune "Emerald" appeared on the top half of page 6 of The Saints' Harmony *with the text on a separate half page (opposite)*

8.

P. M.

BURST ye emerald gates, and bring
To my raptured vision,
All th' ecstatic joys that spring
Round the bright Elysian!
Lo! we lift our longing eyes;
Break the intervening skies;
Sun of Righteousness, arise!
Ope the gates of Paradise.

2 Floods of everlasting light
Freely flash before him;
Myriads, with supreme delight,
Instantly adore him;
Angels' trumps resound his fame;
Lutes of lucid gold proclaim
All the music of his name,
Heaven reverberates the theme.

3 Four and twenty elders rise
From their princely station;
Shout his glorious victories,
Sing his great salvation;
Cast their crowns before his throne;
Cry, in reverential tone,
Glory be to God alone,
Holy! Holy! Holy One!

4 Hark! the thrilling symphonies
Seem, methinks, to seize us;
Join we too the holy lays—
Jesus! Blessed Jesus!
Sweetest sound in Seraphs' song;
Sweetest note on mortal tongue;
Sweetest carol ever sung;
Jesus! Jesus! Holy One!

9.

8s & 7s.

JESUS, hail! enthroned in glory,
There forever to abide;
All the heavenly host adore thee,
Seated at thy Father's side.

2 There for sinners thou art pleading,
There thou dost our place prepare;
Ever for us interceding,
Till in glory we appear.

3 Worship, honor, power, and blessing,
Thou art worthy to receive:
Loudest praises, without ceasing,
Meet it is for us to give.

4 Help, ye bright angelic spirits!
Bring your sweetest, noblest lays;
Help to sing our Savior's merits,—
Help to chant Immanuel's praise.

10.

L. M.

UNMOVED by fear,—my praise is due
To thee, thou gracious God of saints;
Thy mercies great, thy counsel true,
My prayers are heard and my complaints.

2 Compassed by love,—my heart's best thought
I raise in gratitude to thee;
Nor wait to thank thee all untaught,
Thy love's best gift hath taught it me.

3 I fear,—but that I may not gain,
A place beside my noblest friend;
I love,—but ah! the sweet refrain,
On thee, my Savior, I depend.

Blest Be Thou, O God of Israel

THIS BELOVED HYMN is a faithful poetic paraphrase of King David's prayer in I Chronicles 29:10–12. The King James rendering of the prayer is as follows:

> Blessed be thou, Lord God of Israel our father, for ever and ever. Thine, O Lord, is the greatness, and the power, and the glory, and the victory, and the majesty; for all that is in the heaven and in the earth is thine; thine is the kingdom, O Lord, and thou art exalted as head above all. Both riches and honor come of thee, and thou reignest over all; and in thine hand is power and might; and in thine hand it is to make great, and to give strength unto all.

The text of the hymn paraphrase of this scripture is attributed to Henry U. Onderdonk (1789–1858) and is matched in our hymnals with one of Mark Forscutt's loveliest tunes. Forscutt's daughter, Ruby C. Faunce, has written the following account of the unique circumstances surrounding the writing of the tune:

> In the year 1885 or 1886, Father was holding meetings at Pittsburgh, Pennsylvania. It was when he was alone in his room one night about ten o'clock, that he heard beautiful music. His room opened into the hall which led past the room where an hour before he had conducted a preaching service. And as he listened, he thought sure the lady of the house was playing on the piano in the church room.
>
> The music continuing, plainly, clearly, a few moments, father decided to go to the room and see who was playing. On his way he met the sister at whose house he was staying and who offered shelter for the meetings.
>
> "I thought that was you playing, Brother Forscutt!" she gasped.
>
> "And I thought it was you."
>
> Realizing that heavenly influences were about them, they entered the room, and father played the melody from memory, the sister verifying that this was what she had heard. This tune Father named "Norman," and to it we sing in our *Hymnal* the words, "Blest Be Thou, O God of Israel."[31]

This lovely hymn is printed here as it appears in the current hymnal, *Hymns of the Saints*.

PRAISE

24 Blest Be Thou, O God of Israel

I Chronicles 29:10, 11
II Nephi 6:41, 42

NORMAN 8.7.8.7.

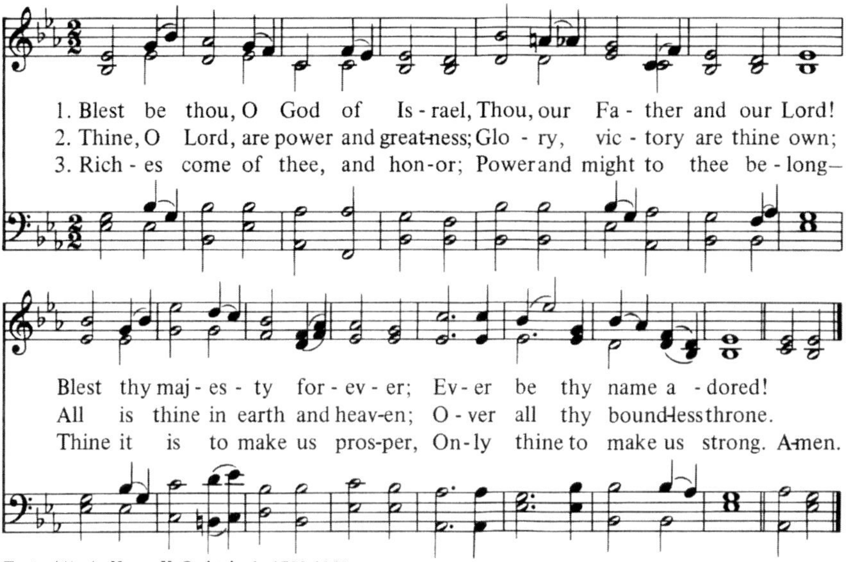

Text: Attr. to Henry U. Onderdonk, 1789-1858.
Tune: Mark H. Forscutt, 1834-1903.

Mark Forscutt (1834–1903)

Shall We Gather Home to Zion

THIS MUCH-LOVED SONG about "the Gathering" was based on a text and tune popular in America in the late nineteenth century. That song, "Shall We Gather at the River," was written in 1864 by Robert Lowry, but for the Reorganization it became "Shall We Gather Home to Zion." This hymn of gathering to the Center Place was sung to the same spirited tune, but with a new text by Thomas Wood Smith.

T. W. Smith was born in Philadelphia and joined the Independent Christian Church at the age of fifteen. At the age of nineteen, he began to preach. While preaching in Iowa, he met Jason Briggs and Israel Rogers, both pioneers of the Reorganization, who proceeded to convert him. As often happened in those days, Smith was baptized and ordained an elder on the same day, and began to serve as a missionary for his new church. In 1873, he was ordained an apostle and accepted missions as far away as Australia and the Society Islands. After being stricken with paralysis in 1892, he finally returned to Independence, the city to which he had longed to gather. Exactly when this hymn was written is not known, but it first appeared in print in 1870 in *The Saints' Harp*. It is reproduced here as it appeared in the 1933 *Saints' Hymnal*.

Christ, the Son

182 BEAUTIFUL RIVER. 8. 7. 8. 7. D. & Refrain.

T. W. Smith, 1838–1894 Robert Lowry, 1864

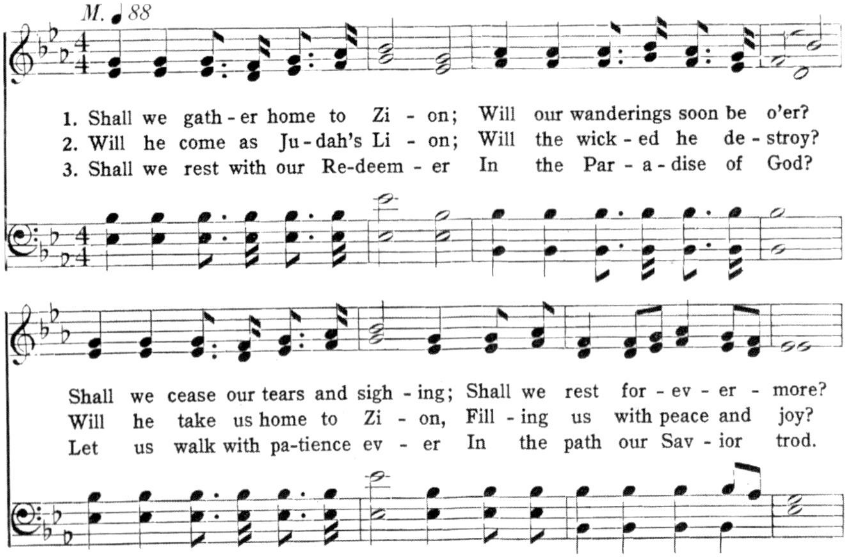

Will Mes - si - ah come to save us From the pow - er of the foe?
Shall we live with him for - ev - er; Shall we see him as he is?
Let us be no lon - ger sleep - ing, For the day is near at hand;
Will he come, and will he have us His sal - va - tion ful - ly know?
Shall we from him part? No, nev - er; He will call each dear one his.
Let us each our watch be keep - ing, As a firm, u - nit - ed band.
Refrain
p
1-2. Yes, we'll gath - er home to Zi - on, Our beau-ti - ful, our beau-ti - ful Zi - on!
3. Then we'll dwell with saints in Zi - on, Our beau-ti - ful, our beau-ti - ful Zi - on!
Gath - er with the saints home to Zi - on, And be saved in the King-dom of God.
Hap - py with the saints home in Zi - on, And re-joice in the King-dom of God.

Yes, We Trust the Day Is Breaking

HERE IS ANOTHER HYMN that was not written by a Latter Day Saint, but was one of those already-existing hymns that must have appealed a great deal to the Saints. It bears a strong testimony that a new day is dawning for the gospel of Jesus Christ as it is preached abroad, in lands far and wide, through the power of God.

The text was written in 1809 by an Irishman, Thomas Kelly, a minister in the Church of Ireland who eventually left the state church to found his own independent group. He was by all accounts a magnetic preacher and a friend to the poor and oppressed. He was also a prolific hymn writer, publishing no fewer than 765 hymn texts in his lifetime, many with his own original music.

Kelly's text appeared in Emma's Nauvoo hymnal, and the 1889 *Saints' Harmony* sets it to an interesting tune, "Calcutta," written by an Englishman named Thomas Clark. Clark was a music leader at the Wesleyan chapel at Canterbury, and later at the Unitarian church in that historic English city. Clark's tune is a stirring and ambitious one that allows the congregation to sing parts as a choir, complete with solo and echo phrases for the various voice parts. Admittedly, this style of music is dated, and while it has all but disappeared from modern hymnals, it can be enjoyable to sing as a charming bit of nostalgia, and as a window to the music of past times.

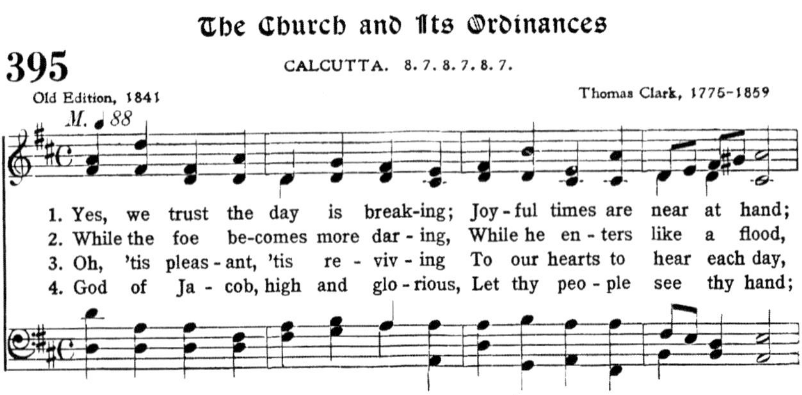

pp
p
ff
God, the might-y God is speak-ing; By his word in ev-ery land,
Christ, the Sav-ior, is pre-par-ing Means to spread his truth a-broad;
Joy-ful news from far ar-riv-ing, How the gos-pel wins its way,
Let the gos-pel be vic-to-rious, Through the world, in ev-ery land,
When he choos-es, When he choos-es, Dark-ness flies at his com-mand,
Ev-ery lan-guage, Ev-ery lan-guage Soon shall tell the love of God,
Those en-light-ening, Those en-light-ening, Who in death and dark-ness lay,
Then shall i-dols, Then shall i-dols Per-ish, Lord, at thy com-mand,
Dark-ness flies at his com-mand, Dark-ness flies at his com-mand,
Dark-ness flies at his com-mand, Dark-ness flies at his com-mand, Dark-ness flies at his com-mand,
Soon shall tell the love of God, Soon shall tell the love of God,
Soon shall tell the love of God, Soon shall tell the love of God, Soon shall tell the love of God,
Who in death and dark-ness lay, Who in death and dark-ness lay,
Who in death and dark-ness lay, Who in death and dark-ness lay, Who in death and dark-ness lay,
Per-ish, Lord, at thy com-mand, Per-ish, Lord, at thy com-mand,
Per-ish, Lord, at thy com-mand, Per-ish, Lord, at thy com-mand, Per-ish, Lord, at thy com-mand,
Dark-ness flies at his com-mand.
Soon shall tell the love of God.
Who in death and dark-ness lay.
Per-ish, Lord, at thy com-mand.

The original 1903 pipe organ in the Stone Church in Independence, Missouri

God has spoken from on high,
this the light, this the light,
And now bids the world come nigh
to this light of God
Carrie Thomas, 1895 *Saints' Hymnal,* number 182

VI. The Saints' Hymnal of 1895

At the Conference of 1895, a resolution initiated by the St. Louis District was accepted that set forth a remarkably detailed plan for a new hymnal that would avoid the problems of *The Saints' Harmony.* The resolution recommended a procedure for quickly obtaining suggestions of most-used hymns and tunes from the branches. It went on to specify that the new book should be a "smaller and more convenient" volume, with no more than two hundred hymns, plus fifty additional numbers to be "grouped in the back of the work with one bar of the tune above." The book should be called "The Saints' Hymnal," and should be priced at "not more than fifty cents each." The resolution even suggested the names of three musicians, Ralph G. Smith, Lucy L. Resseguie, and Arthur H. Mills, to serve as a committee to compile the book.[32] Mark Forscutt's name was not among them.

In a short time, the 1895 *Saints' Hymnal* was published in Lamoni, Iowa, the church headquarters at the time. The collection was, for all intents and purposes, an abridgement of Forscutt's *Saints' Harmony.* The committee presented the following statement as their preface to the book, addressing the instructions of the conference, and also making reference to liberties Mark Forscutt had taken with some of the musical settings in the *Harmony*:

> TO THE CHURCH: Your committee herewith presents the "SAINTS' HYMNAL," made up largely of selections from the "HARMONY," together with some tunes of recognized merit from other works. We have

> corrected errors in harmony, where such existed in the original tunes, and have submitted the matter to a competent master in harmony for his final correction. Those which were not original, but had been taken from other works have, when necessary, been restored as they were written. We have endeavored to do our work according to the spirit of our instructions, and trust it will meet with your approval.[33]

In their work, the committee managed to fulfill each of the requirements stated by the conference, including the suggestion that each hymn tune be referenced with its page number in *The Saints' Harmony*, and each text referenced with its source in *The Saints' Harp*. One exception seems to be that evidently 250 hymns was found to be too limiting, since the total number included was actually 300, with yet more hymns being added in subsequent editions.[34] As was suggested by the conference action, the back portion of the book contained a number of hymn texts printed with only the initial few bars of the suggested tune given. However, most of the selections were printed in what we now consider to be the normal fashion, with texts placed between the two staves of music throughout.

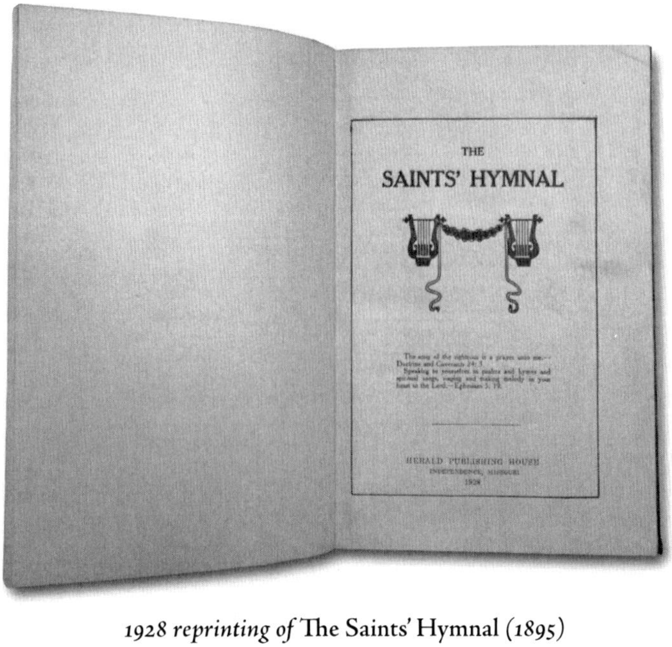

1928 reprinting of The Saints' Hymnal *(1895)*

HYMNS FROM *THE SAINTS' HYMNAL* OF 1895

'Tis a Glorious Thing to Be in the Light

THE REORGANIZATION CONTINUED to celebrate the uniqueness of the Restoration message, including concepts such as the one true church restored from days of old, the gifts of the gospel through prophetic revelation, and the imminent return of Christ. The core of this message could be encapsulated in the idea of light coming into a world of darkness through the unique truths of the gospel. This message found expression in a hymn by Carrie A. Church, which begins, "'Tis a glorious thing to be in the Light."

The Church family discovered the Book of Mormon while Carrie was a child. They believed its message, but never made contact with the church. Years later, when Carrie married, she shared her beliefs with her husband, and they eventually wrote to Joseph Smith at Plano, Illinois, in 1867, asking for baptism. As a result, Apostle E. C. Briggs was dispatched to Michigan, where the family was living at the time. After a series of meetings, Briggs baptized the family and began the work of establishing a new branch in that area.

The story is told that as Carrie was going about her housework one day, the words of this hymn formed in her mind. She was in the final stages of pregnancy at the time, and only a few hours after she completed the writing of these words she gave birth to twin girls. This hymn text, Carrie Church's affirmation of the glorious light of the gospel, was printed in the 1870 *Saints' Harp*. In the 1889 *Saints' Harmony*, it was set to a tune by William Bradbury, a prominent hymn writer of the nineteenth century, and it continued to be paired with this tune in the next two hymnals of the church. *The Hymnal* of 1956, however, altered the initial word from "'Tis" to "What," and included it in its historical section as well as in the main body of the hymnal, where it was set to a more conservative tune written for it by Franklyn S. Weddle and Evan Fry. The hymn is reproduced here as it appeared in the 1895 *Saints' Hymnal*.

116 SAINTS' HYMNAL.
182 (1078) IN THE LIGHT. P. M. (S. H. 524)
WM. B. BRADBURY.
m
p
pp
1. 'Tis a glo - rious thing to be, In the light, in the light,
2. Long the earth in dark-ness lay, With-out light, with-out light,
3. Proph - ets are re - stored a - gain, In the light, in the light,
4. Let us keep our spir - its pure, In the light, in the light,
m
mp
Which the saints of old did see, The true light of God;
But the dark - ness fled a - way, Before the light of God.
And the gos - pel gifts to men, In the light of God;
And un - to the end en - dure, In the light of God;
m
p
pp
Rev - e - la - tion's ho - ly light, Is the light, is the light,
God has spok - en from on high, This the light, this the light,
Bless - ings to the an - cients giv'n, In the light, in the light,
Then when Je - sus comes a - gain, In the light, in the light,
m
mp
And all else is dark as night, Save this light of God.
And now bids the world come nigh, To this light of God.
Are a - gain re - ceived from heav'n, In the light of God.
We shall live and with him reign, In the light of God.

"'Tis a Glorious Thing to Be in the Light" as it appeared in the 1895 Saints' Hymnal.

The Old Stone Church in Plano, Illinois

Book of Mormon, Hid for Ages

The Book of Mormon was valued by the Reorganization as unique and important scripture, as it had been since the beginning of the movement. Several expressions of this conviction emerged in the form of hymns, including a two-stanza text by Joseph Smith III:

Ah, Book of Mormon! Golden Book,
The book of precious promise,
Whoe'er, in faith, shall in thee look,
Shall drink from golden chalice.

No happier rules of life are found,
Upon the Bible's pages,
Than those which in this book abound,
The book of former ages.

One of the most popular of the hymns on this theme, however, was the hymn "Book of Mormon, Hid for Ages," written in 1867 by H. S. Dille.

In the early years of the Reorganization, Plano, Illinois, filled the role of being the primary congregation of the church. The publishing plant was set up there in 1863, and two years later Joseph III moved his family to Plano. Harvey S. Dille was a church member who was employed at the publishing plant. He had a strong conviction of the truths of the gospel, except for some misgivings about the Book of Mormon. He asked for prayers that he would have a testimony concerning the book, and in due time this came to be his experience. One day at a prayer service in Plano, Dille stood and bore his testimony of the book, and then sang the hymn he had been inspired to write.

Dille's verses first appeared in the 1870 *Saints' Harp*, and in the 1889 *Saints' Harmony* it was set to an original tune by Mark Forscutt. The spirited tune to which this hymn has been sung since that time was written by the nineteenth-century American tune writer Thomas Hastings, who is reputed to have written one thousand hymn tunes during his lifetime. The hymn appears here as it was printed in the 1933 *Saints' Hymnal.*

The Church and Its Ordinances

403

ZION. 8. 7. 8. 7. 4. 7. 4. 7.

H. S. Dille, 1867 — Dr. Thomas Hastings, 1830

God Is Marshalling His Army

In recent years, references to militarism have all but disappeared from our hymns, but in the past, poets and other people of faith tended to portray the committed Christian as analogous to a soldier fighting a fierce battle. The apostle Paul speaks in these terms in Ephesians 6:10–17, no doubt giving inspiration for the famous hymn, "Onward Christian Soldiers." This hymn, "God Is Marshalling His Army," would be another good example of this analogy. The text is replete with the imagery of battles, valor, and victory won.

The author of the text, Joseph Woodward, was born in Staffordshire, England, and emigrated to America during the early years of the Reorganization. Upon settling in New England, he came in contact with the church appointee for that area, T. W. Smith (the same person who authored "Shall We Gather Home to Zion," mentioned earlier). Little else is known about the life of the hymn's author, apart from the record of his baptism at East Boston in 1867 and his ordination to the office of elder in 1870 at the Fall River, Massachusetts, congregation.

For several years, this hymn was sung to the same tune used for "Jesus, I My Cross Have Taken," but for the *Saints' Harmony* of 1889, Mark Forscutt asked a church member musician, Henry R. Mills, to write a more stirring, march-like tune for it. Mills had been born near Kirtland, Ohio, in 1844, where his parents had earlier united with the church. Soon after the martyrdom of Joseph and Hyrum Smith, however, while Henry was still an infant, the family moved to Pittsfield, Illinois. In 1875, Mark Forscutt came to Pittsfield to hold preaching services, and the following year, after several months of contemplation, Henry Mills was baptized into the Reorganization. In 1884, the family gathered to Independence, Missouri, where Henry became active in the music of both the church and community. He was ordained a member of the high council of the newly organized Independence Stake in 1901.

Several members of the Mills family made substantial contributions to the hymnody of the Reorganization. One of Henry's sons, Arthur, was mentioned earlier as a member of the 1895 *Saints' Hymnal* committee, and is the composer of several hymn tunes, including two found in *Hymns of the Saints*. One of his tunes, called "James," is sung with "How Gentle God's Commands" (HS 130), and the other, "Hicks," is used for

"With Thankful Hearts We Meet" (HS 3), and "Lord God, We Meet in Jesus' Name" (HS 365). Henry's son Frank is the author of the fine Christmas hymn text, "Newborn of God" (HS 247).

"God Is Marshalling His Army" was first published in the 1870 and 1889 hymnals edited by Mark Forscutt. It is printed on the following page exactly as it appeared in the 1895 *Saints' Hymnal,* set to Henry Mills's tune "Pittsfield," which he named for the town where he joined the Reorganization.

The original 1881 offices of the Herald Publishing House in Lamoni, showing the 1894 addition. This structure burned on January 5, 1907, but was replaced by year's end.

"God Is Marshalling His Army," reproduced as it appeared in the 1895 Saints' Hymnal

Gladly I join in the triumphant song,
Tenderly, tenderly, leading me on.

Joseph Smith III, *Zion's Praises*, number 5

VII. *Zion's Praises*, 1903

DURING THE PERIOD at the turn of the century, the Sunday School movement had been spreading throughout the church, along with a "Religio Society" for youth. Responding to the urging of the General Sunday School Association, a committee was appointed to prepare, as a supplement to *The Saints' Hymnal*, a songbook that would be better suited to these activities. Thus, in 1903, a collection of 232 musical compositions, primarily lively assembly songs and gospel hymns, was published in Lamoni under the name, *Zion's Praises*. The committee consisted of F. G. Pitt, Audentia Anderson, Viola Blair, Vida E. Smith, and Aletha May White. In its introductory paragraph to the book, the Board of Publication stated, in part:

> Zion's Praises is sent out with the hope that it will meet a hearty welcome from all lovers of the beautiful in music and song . . . With a desire to help the song service of the Sabbath-schools everywhere, interest the young, gladden the hearts of the elderly, and honor in grateful praise God, to whom all honor and exaltation is fully due, the work is submitted and dedicated to Zion's hopeful children.[35]

As the committee hoped, the new hymnal soon found acceptance not only by the young, but by many older members as well. Many of the hymns were drawn from popular gospel hymnals of the day, the product of authors and composers such as Fanny Crosby and Ira D. Sankey, and although most of these are today considered to be overly sentimental, a few, such as Charles H. Gabriel's "Great and Marvelous Are Thy Works," have survived as favorites in the current hymnal. A number of new original works were also presented, including one particular hymn from among several that had recently been written in Lamoni by two members of the committee, Vida Smith and Audentia Smith Anderson.

Hymns from *Zion's Praises*, 1903

There's an Old, Old Path

Vida E. Smith, daughter of Alexander Hale and Elizabeth Kendall Smith, and her cousin Audentia Smith Anderson, daughter of Joseph III and Bertha Madison Smith, combined their talents in the writing of several hymns, including the first hymn in *Zion's Praises*, "One Day When Fell the Spirit's Whisper," which has the gift of song as its theme. Vida was the poet and Audentia was the musician. But it was another of their efforts that produced what is arguably the best-loved hymn ever to come forth from the Reorganization. Here is the often-told story of how "The Old, Old Path" was written, from the author's own accounts.

One Sunday morning, Vida Smith sat in the old Brick Church in Lamoni and listened as the speaker began his sermon, using the text from Jeremiah 6:16: "Thus saith the Lord, 'Stand ye in the ways, and see, and ask for the old paths, where is the good way, and walk therein.'" Smith immediately "tuned out," and began contemplating the meaning of that scripture. She wrote:

> [The speaker] soon faded from my realization as my eyes rested on the swaying branches of the trees outside and the soft clouds against the blue sky, and I felt the nearness of congenial friends. I felt at home in the house of God and I felt at ease before his mercy seat. The glory of the message of the ancient prophet flooded my soul and opening my quarterly I wrote on the fly-leaf the words of the song exactly as they appear in the [hymnal].[36]

The sermon and even the name of the speaker that morning have been long forgotten, but during that hour of worship was born a hymn that most members of Community of Christ can still sing from memory more than a century later. "The Old, Old Path" continues to be an inspiring and eloquent expression of the treasure of close companionship with good friends and with the Master.

This hymn is reproduced here exactly as it first appeared, in *Zion's Praises* of 1903.

No. 207. The Old, Old Path.

VIDA E. SMITH. M. A. ANDERSON.

Tenderly, Tenderly

THIS HYMN IS among the four poems by Joseph Smith III that continue to be sung today by Community of Christ. Throughout his lifetime, the prophet experienced the loss of an unusually large number of family members, experiences that sorely tried his faith over a considerable length of time. The loss of two children was followed by the death of his first wife, Emmaline, and then, a few years later, by the loss of his eldest son, David Carlos. But it was when his youngest daughter, Bertha Azuba, was killed in a tragic school playground accident that his grief became inconsolable. He had been away from home in the service of his God, and while he was thus engaged in ministry one of his dearest treasures had been taken from him, and in such a tragic way.

It was at the point when his grief became almost unbearable that he received a particularly deep spiritual experience that eventually helped him to reconcile his loss. Even the prophet of the church was not to be spared the sorrows of life. But, through the grace of a loving God, he was able to emerge from this time of anguish offering a greater, deeper ministry to his people.

It was out of experiences such as this that the hymn "Tenderly, Tenderly," was written. Stanza one is a sincere and honest expression of doubt and struggle, and the original stanza two (dropped in *Hymns of the Saints*), is a prayer for strength. Then, stanza three appears with an uplifting sense of triumph in the face of despair: "Now has my weak heart grown trustingly strong; Ways have grown short that seemed once to be long; Gladly I join in the triumphant song; Tenderly, tenderly, leading me on."

One Sunday after a service in the old Brick Church in Lamoni, Joseph stopped his friend Norman W. Smith and gave him a copy of this hymn, requesting that he write a tune for it, as he had for other poems by the prophet (see "Let Us Breathe One Fervent Prayer," HS 482). It has been sung to Norman Smith's tune ever since.

This historic hymn is printed here just as it appeared in the 1903 *Zion's Praises*.

No. 5. Tenderly Lead Thou Me On.

JOSEPH SMITH. N. W. SMITH.

I Have Found the Glorious Gospel

One morning in the late 1800s, James Edwards, a church member living in Boston, was greeted by a curious question from his wife. Arriving at the breakfast table, she inquired of him the meaning of the word "Eureka." He replied that it was a Greek word meaning "I have found." She told him she had dreamed that they were at a church meeting, and she had seen him opening a hymnal and saying "Sing Eureka." They looked through several hymn books, but could find no hymn by that name, and the experience was soon forgotten.

From time to time, Edwards tried his hand at writing original poetry, and he kept a collection of his verses for his own use. One day, he sat down at his desk and decided to send off a contribution to the new church-sponsored college in Iowa, Graceland College. And, since the *Saints' Herald* was being published in Lamoni at the time, he decided to enclose a poem he had written, asking that it be forwarded to the editor of that magazine. The poem was centered around the theme of the angel message, and as he prepared the letter for mailing, he looked down and noticed the opening words, "I have found." He remembered with astonishment his wife's dream, and the word "Eureka."

The poem was, in fact, printed in the *Herald*, and became a favorite hymn of many Saints in the ensuing years. The tune to which it was sung (appropriately named "The Angel Message") was written specifically for this text by Henry R. Mills, mentioned earlier as the composer of the tune for "God Is Marshalling His Army." This hymn is reproduced here as it appeared in the 1903 *Zion's Praises*.

No. 206. The Angel Message.

James L. Edwards. H. R. Mills.

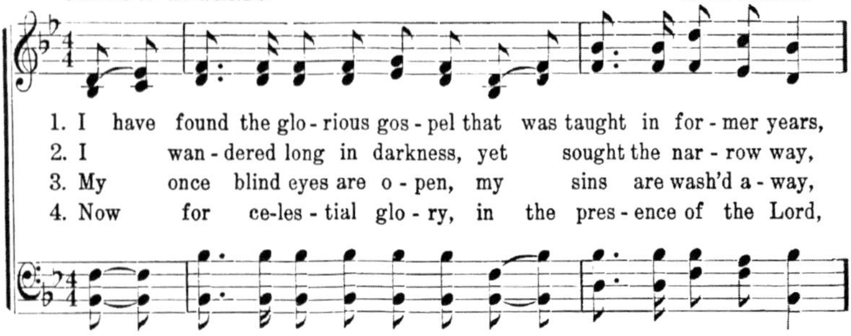

With its gifts and bless - ings all so full and free; And my
And my life was like the surg - ing of the sea; But
And the King - dom I can ve - ry plain - ly see; No
I will work and watch and hum - bly bow the knee; No
soul is thrill'd with glad - ness, and ban- ished are my fears, Since the
now I am re - joic - ing in this the lat - ter day, Since the
more do fears and doubt - ings my trust - ing soul dis - may, Since the
long - er faith, but knowl - edge, in true and sweet ac - cord, With the
CHORUS.
pre - cious An - gel Mes-sage came to me.
pre - cious An - gel Mes-sage came to me. Then praise the Lord, oh, my
pre - cious An - gel Mes-sage came to me.
pre - cious An - gel Mes-sage bro't to me.
soul! A - bun-dant mer-cy, oh, how free! In joy - ful song Thy
Spir - it doth ac - cord, Since the pre - cious An - gel Mes-sage came to me.

Zion's Praises "Gospel" Hymns

As has been mentioned, the 1903 *Zion's Praises* included not only original hymns like those discussed above, but also many evangelical Christian hymns written in what is known as the popular "gospel" style of the time. Typically, these hymns contained rather basic theology and were set to music either sentimental or lively in style (often both). Many of these were dropped from subsequent hymnals of the church. Of course, these songs had been selected with the general Sunday School movement in mind, and were meant to be immediately appealing to people of all ages. As examples of songs in this style, three hymns are reproduced on the following pages, as they appeared in *Zion's Praises*:

1. **"Trust and Obey,"** with a text written in 1887 by Presbyterian minister John H. Sammis and a tune by Methodist minister and musician, Daniel B. Towner.

2. **"Are You Witnessing for Him?"** ("Tell Me, Brother, Worn and Weary"). This vigorous hymn by Alice Batchelder and James H. Fillmore features what is known as a "patter chorus" on the refrain. The melody stretches out the text, while the lower voices sing a repeated or faster-moving text, resulting in a kind of enthusiastic "patter."

3. **"We're Marching to Zion"** ("Come Ye That Love the Lord"), with a 1707 Isaac Watts text set in 1867 to music with an added refrain by Baptist minister and musician Robert Lowry.

Zion's Praises (1903)

No. 4. Trust and Obey.

Rev. J. H. Sammis. D. B. Towner.

No. 201. Are You Witnessing for Him?

ALICE M. BATCHELDER. J. H. FILLMORE.

Are You Witnessing for Him?

No. 37. We're Marching to Zion.

Isaac Watts. Rev. Robert Lowry.

Onward to Zion, march on with a song,
Zion the beautiful beckons us on.

F. M. Smith, 1933 *Saints' Hymnal,* number 436

VIII. The Saints' Hymnal of 1933

DURING THE FIRST three decades of the twentieth century there were two hymnals, the 1903 *Zion's Praises* and the 1895 *Saints' Hymnal,* in concurrent use throughout the church, and it was generally felt that it would be more practical to combine selections from both books into a single volume. Responding to surveys of preferences from among the membership, a committee led by musicians Paul Craig and Evan Fry chose 442 hymns from the two books as well as several other sources. The new hymnal was published in 1933, continuing the use of the name *The Saints' Hymnal.* This is the venerable "old blue hymnal" so fondly remembered today by many Saints who grew up singing from it.

Of the three hymns from the 1933 hymnal that are discussed on the following pages, two were new to that volume, while one had appeared earlier in *Zion's Praises.* All three have their own significance to the story of hymnody in the Reorganization.

These early years of the twentieth century saw the church beginning to make strides in the coordination of its music ministry. Frederick M. Smith, then a counselor in the First Presidency, met with a number of the church's musicians for this purpose during the Conference of 1912. From this effort, the "general choir" movement was organized under the enthusiastic leadership of Albert N. Hoxie. In advance of the next conference, singers from a number of the larger branches rehearsed several selected anthems in their separate locations and came together to sing them for the conference. This success led to more challenging works, including cantatas and oratorios, and, in 1916, the first of what would become the annual performances of Handel's *Messiah*, which continue to this day. Eventually, the "general choir" movement led to the establishment in 1920 of a Department of Music for the church. All this activity was largely voluntary, however, and it would be twenty-four years before a full-time director of music would be appointed.

Hymns from *The Saints' Hymnal*, 1933

Onward to Zion

Following the death of Joseph Smith III in 1914, the mantle of prophetic leadership fell to his eldest son, Frederick Madison Smith. "F. M.," as he was called, had been born at Plano, Illinois, in 1874, and moved with his family and the headquarters of the church to Lamoni, Iowa when he was seven years old. After a year at the University of Iowa, he returned to Lamoni to become the first graduate of Graceland College in 1898. In 1915, he was awarded a Ph.D. from Clark University in Massachusetts, writing his dissertation on "The Higher Powers of Man."

Frederick Madison assumed the leadership of the denomination during a period of tension and change in the church as a whole, as well as in the leading quorums. This was reflected in the Conference of 1922, when the document that was to become Section 134 was approved only after ten days of consideration, and with a vote of 656 to 452. One evening during the Conference, President Smith was sitting alone in his living room, listening to a recording of Stephen Foster's "Beautiful Dreamer." As he sat contemplating the future of the church, and with Foster's tune in his mind, the words of this hymn were formulated. It is F. M. Smith's expression of hope for the church he loved so much, and for the realization of the Zionic community in which he believed so fervently.

For *The Hymnal* of 1956, this hymn with its original tune was placed in the section for historic hymns, while it appeared in the main body of the hymnal set to a new, more traditional hymn tune written for it by Franklyn S. Weddle. It is reproduced here with the Stephen Foster melody, as it appeared in the 1933 *Saints' Hymnal*.

436

ONWARD TO ZION. Irregular.

Frederick M. Smith

Foster
Arranged by Helen Silsbee Smith

"*Onward to Zion*" *from the* 1933 Saints' Hymnal

We Limit Not the Truth of God

IT HAS BEEN said that, although this hymn text was not written by a Latter Day Saint, it should have been. In these verses, the Englishman George Rawson has caught up well the essence of the Restoration movement's emphasis on continuing revelation. It is a message that is ever new and ever needed. We must not bind by our limited understanding the infinite truths that wait to be revealed.

Because of the importance of these words, it is fitting that we should sing them to a tune written by a member of the Reorganization. The name of the tune, "Hills," was the maiden name of its composer, Louise Hills Lewis. She was born in 1887 at Cedar Rapids, Iowa, and studied music as a child, including piano, organ, voice, harmony, and conducting. In later years especially, she would put her musical training to active use in the service of the church. In addition to this music, she wrote a number of other hymn tunes, including the tune "Confirmation," used today for "Here at the Water's Brink We Stand" (HS 354), and "Behold Thy Sons and Daughters, Lord" (HS 361).

This hymn is reproduced here as it first appeared, in the 1933 *Saints' Hymnal*.

Vida Smith (1865–1945) and Audentia Anderson (1872–1963)

Revelation and Restoration

416

HILLS. C. M. D.

G. Rawson, 1807–1889 Louise Hills Lewis, 1887—

It May Not Be on the Mountain's Height (I'll Go Where You Want Me to Go)

THIS HYMN FIRST appeared in our hymnals in the *Zion's Praises* of 1903, and continued in the 1933 *Saints' Hymnal* and *The Hymnal* of 1956. It was not written by a Latter Day Saint, but nevertheless became an important hymn for the church due to its special role in General Conferences. For a number of years this hymn, with its key line, "I'll go where you want me to go, dear Lord," was sung at the end of the conferences, when the appointee assignments were read and the missionary ministers filled the stage of the Auditorium. These were emotional moments because, during those years, the assignments had not previously been disclosed, either to the church or to the ministers themselves.

The authorship of this text has been a matter of controversy. Attributed to an otherwise unknown "Mary Brown," some scholars feel that it was actually written by Charles H. Gabriel, who used a number of pseudonyms for the many hymns he wrote. (As an example, both the text and tune of the well-known hymn "Great and Marvelous Are Thy Works" were written by Gabriel, although the text is credited to a "Charlotte G. Homer.") In any case, stanzas two and three of "I'll Go Where You Want Me to Go" appear to have been written by someone else altogether, the late-nineteenth-century hymn writer Charles Prior. The tune to which this hymn has always been sung was written specifically for it by Carrie E. Rounsefell.

As *The Hymnal* of 1956 was being compiled, the committee felt that this hymn tended to limit the appreciation of ministry to those who could "go," as opposed to those who would "stay" and minister where they resided. Consequentially, a new hymn was written by Evan Fry and Franklyn Weddle and included in that hymnal. The new hymn, "From Isles and Continents Afar," includes the line, "I'll go or stay, nor count the cost, Thy people serve where'er they be."

"I'll Go Where You Want Me to Go" is reproduced here as it appeared in the 1933 *Saints' Hymnal.*

Loyalty—Devotion—Consecration

292

I'LL GO WHERE YOU WANT ME TO GO. Irregular & Refrain.

Mary Brown Carrie E. Rounsefell

The Saints' Hymnal (1933)

The Hymnal (1956)

With hymns of praise we worship thee,
O God of harmony;
Our gifts of music bring, and pray
That pleasing they may be.
Evan Fry, *The Hymnal,* number 506

IX. Franklyn Weddle and The Hymnal, 1956

In 1943, a highly significant event in the musical life of the church occurred when a musician who had been teaching in Flint, Michigan, accepted the role of an appointee minister in the RLDS Church. Franklyn S. Weddle became the first person to assume full-time leadership of the music and worship life of the denomination. President F. M. Smith had recognized that it was time for the church to set up a department of music, but other church leaders feared the appointment of "specialists." Thus, Weddle's initial assignment was to serve as pastor of the Central Congregation in Kansas City, Missouri, for one year, after which he would organize a "General Church music department."[37]

Franklyn Weddle soon demonstrated that he possessed a rare combination of musical talent, administrative ability, and ministerial capacity. During his twenty-six-year tenure as church music director, he led the church in major advances in the quality and depth of all aspects of music and worship. The annual nationwide broadcast of Handel's *Messiah* reached new heights of excellence, the Independence Symphony Orchestra was founded, a 113-rank Aeolian-Skinner organ was added to the newly completed conference chamber at the headquarters' Auditorium, musicians throughout the church were organized and offered new opportunities to improve the quality of their work, and the number and availability of resources for the task were significantly expanded. In addition to a major new hymnal for the church, discussed below, the music department under Weddle's leadership also published a *Book of Little Hymns*, a *Children's Hymnal*, a *Hymnal for Youth* (in conjunction with a similar publication by The Westminster Press) and a *Camp and Fellowship Song Book*.

One of Weddle's major goals in upgrading the quality of music in the church was the compilation of a new hymnal with elevated musical and theological standards. In 1950 a new hymnal committee began its work, and this time the group consisted not only of musicians, but also pastors, missionaries, teachers, writers, theologians, and church administrators. The illustrious list included, in addition to Weddle, the following names: Paul Craig, Alice Edwards, Mabel Carlile Hyde, Evan Fry, Roy Cheville, Henry Livingston, Arthur Oakman, Herbert Lively, Chris Hartshorn, and Harold Neal (all are pictured on p. 89). The result of their efforts, a new collection of 583 hymns titled simply *The Hymnal*, was published in 1956. The goals of this work were summarized by Weddle:

> The committee has endeavored to maintain a high standard for both words and music, without becoming too stilted or formal. Hymns have been chosen not only for their emotional qualities, but for poetical excellence, musical quality, doctrinal soundness, and such other qualities as would promote dignity, order, and true reverence in worship.[38]

In the application of these standards, many of the more sentimental, toe-tapping gospel hymns, with their often repetitive texts and questionable or shallow theology, were abandoned (to the dismay of some of the membership). Along with hymns from other denominations, twenty-nine new tunes and forty-six new texts by RLDS members appeared for the first time in *The Hymnal*. Many of these were specifically written to meet identified needs, such as the need for hymns concerning the sacraments. Still other hymns were revised to better reflect current doctrinal and musical standards. Among the advances of this collection was the degree of thought and organization it demonstrated, including an extensive array of helpful indexes. The desire to include several hymns from the church's heritage that would not meet the new standards was accommodated by adding an appendix of "Historical Hymns" in the back. Included in this historical section was the legendary LDS hymn "Come, Come, Ye Saints," written in southern Iowa on the trek to Utah. Even though it did not include the verse about finding a place in the

West, the hymn was nevertheless deleted entirely by action of the 1958 World Conference, requested by the Utah–Southeast Idaho District.[39] The church was still concerned about the distinction between the two denominations.

The higher standards of musical and theological integrity set by the committee brought about a number of changes in *The Hymnal*. For example, hymn tunes in the straightforward chordal style of the classical chorale were favored over the more rhythmically driven, repetitive gospel-style tunes. The committee also gave careful attention to ensure that the message of each hymn text was compatible with current beliefs. This point was held to be an important one. Since the RLDS Church/Community of Christ is a church without a formal creed, it can be argued that the hymns of the church have, down through time, served to fill that particular role.

An interesting anecdote in the history of *The Hymnal* concerns the fact that, in later printings of the book, a few contemporary authors were allowed to make "second-thought" alterations in their texts. Even though it may have led to a slight improvement in several hymns, this permission was later regretted when several branches that happened to own different editions of the book experienced the disconcerting effect that resulted when part of the congregation tried to sing one version of a particular hymn while the rest held forth on a different rendering.

Hymns from *The Hymnal*, 1956

Ye Wondering Nations, Now Give Ear

In an effort to upgrade the musical content of *The Hymnal*, Franklyn Weddle took the initiative of writing new tunes for a number of existing hymns that needed more appropriate musical settings. A total of fifteen tunes in that collection are credited to him, with four of them being written in conjunction with Evan Fry. However, it is perhaps the one hymn for which he wrote both text and tune that has come to be most closely associated with this key figure in the Reorganization. That hymn, "Church of Christ, in Latter Days," is the author's eloquent challenge to the church, as relevant today as it was half a century ago. Along with most of Weddle's tunes, this hymn continues to be included in *Hymns of the Saints*, but since access to that current hymnal is readily available, one of the hymns that has not been carried over has been included here.

The text, "Ye Wondering Nations, Now Give Ear," originated in the hymnal published in Manchester, England, in 1840, discussed earlier. The authorship of the text is unknown, and when it appeared in hymnals of the Reorganization, the citation given was simply, "European Edition." The hymn was enthusiastically embraced as a strong affirmation of some of the unique beliefs of the church, including the angel message, the bringing forth of ancient scripture, the coming gathering of modern-day Israel, and the subsequent Zionic reign. The text had appeared in the Reorganization hymnals of 1870, 1889, 1895, and 1933, but it was felt that more suitable music was needed for the 1956 hymnal. As he did so often in his role of church music director and chair of the 1956 hymnal committee, Franklyn Weddle filled this need himself by writing the tune he called "Angel's Cry."

This hymn is reproduced here as it appeared in *The Hymnal* of 1956, often referred to as "the grey hymnal."

The CHURCH and the SACRAMENTS
Revelation and Restoration

286

Angel's Cry C.M.D.
M. ♩ 108

Rev. 14: 6, 7
I Nephi 4: 16
D. and C. 26: 3

European Edition, 1840

Franklyn S. Weddle, 1950

The Morning Stars Together Sang

For many years, Evan Fry was the radio voice of the Reorganized Church. Born into the appointee family of Charles Fry, himself a hymn author (see "O Lord, How Can It Be," number 332 in *Hymns of the Saints*), Evan lived in several cities of the Midwest before settling down in Independence, Missouri, in 1912. His musical training came in addition to his formal schooling, and included private piano lessons and years of singing in various choirs. He did editorial work on the 1933 *Saints' Hymnal*, and began to also do radio work for the church until the Great Depression eliminated his position. He was able to find commercial work in radio in nearby Kansas for several years until the church was in a position to call him back to Independence. He was named director of the church's broadcasting department and later was appointed as the official radio minister. While working in the radio office, Fry became a close friend of Franklyn Weddle, and the two collaborated on many projects, including a number of hymns and hymn tunes.

For many years the church broadcast short morning devotional programs live from a radio studio and transmitter at the Stone Church. The story is told that on more than one occasion during times of severe weather, Fry was the only person able to get to the studio in time for the broadcast. His unusual range of talents enabled him to single-handedly start up the equipment, play the theme music on the organ, sing the solo to his own accompaniment, and preach the morning sermon.

Evan Fry was responsible for no fewer than eleven texts in *The Hymnal* of 1956, for which he served on the selection committee. Again, most of these are so relevant today that they continue to appear in the current hymnal of the church, so we have chosen to include here one that was not continued. This is a text that celebrates the gift of music as it has been displayed through the ages, from the beginning of creation itself. The music for this hymn was written by former Graceland University music faculty member Oliver Houston, Jr.

The hymn is printed here as it appeared in *The Hymnal* of 1956.

SPECIAL SUBJECTS and OCCASIONS
Ministry of Music

D. and C. 110: 23
Matt. 26: 27
Ps. 107: 31, 32

Slover C.M.

M. ♩ 96

506

Evan A. Fry, 1955

Oliver Houston, Jr.

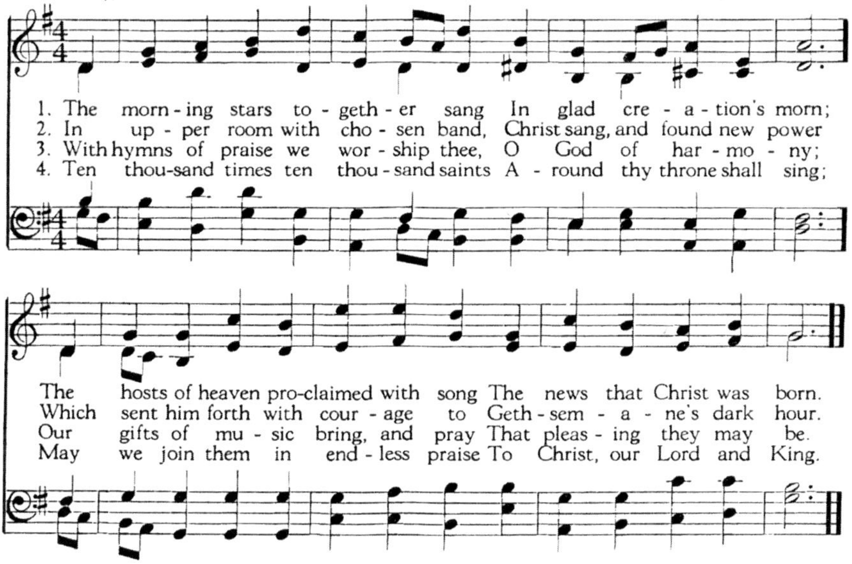

For many years, the church broadcast radio programming from the Stone Church in Independence, Missouri

Send Forth Thy Light, O Zion

THIS HYMN WAS referenced earlier as an example of evolving concepts of Zion throughout the 150 years of the Reorganization. In these verses, Zion is seen not as a particular location where Saints would gather for safety, but rather as an ensign or beacon, out of which light, love, and life would go to all the world.

Of the many legendary individuals who have appeared during the relatively brief history of the Reorganization, perhaps none have been more influential or revered than Roy A. Cheville. He taught and inspired thousands of future leaders of the church in his long-held role of professor of religion and campus pastor at Graceland College, and those years of teaching became significant in helping the church mature in its theological understandings. Despite the heavy demands of his teaching and pastoring, he found time to write numerous articles, books, and hymns. Many of his hymns were written because he could not find anything that was "just right" for the carefully planned worship services of the campus congregation. His work at Graceland came to a close in 1958, when he was called to church appointment to succeed Elbert A. Smith as Presiding Patriarch. In this new role, his singular ministry came to be shared more directly with the church at large.

"Doc" Cheville's ministry was a strong and enthusiastic one that emphasized "doing." In both his speaking and his writing, he preferred words with the more active "ing" ending. His song leading was renowned for its dynamic fervor, almost in the style of an evangelistic cheerleader. Those who sang under his leadership knew they had to sing with all the passion they could muster, and their experience was enhanced by doing so.

A total of eighteen hymn texts in *The Hymnal* were written or revised by Roy Cheville. Some of these have been further revised in *Hymns of the Saints* in order to soften the impact of the strong, masculine language that Cheville favored. And, "Send Forth Thy Light, O Zion," reproduced here as it appears in *The Hymnal* of 1956, has been revised in the 1981 *Hymns of the Saints* to portray a more inclusive spirit. Compare the language in the second stanza of the earlier version, on page 90, with the more inclusive language of the 1981 revision, which reads as follows: (revisions in italics).

Send forth thy love, O Zion! *Thy call is from above,*
To make on earth incarnate *Christ's sacrificial love.*
For *by the* saints outreaching To those their lives can bless
Shall come Zionic witness To heal earth's brokenness.
(1981 *Hymns of the Saints* revision)

In both hymnals, Cheville's text is paired with the vigorous tune "Lancashire" from the nineteenth-century British composer, Henry Smart.

The committee for The Hymnal *of 1956 was a virtual "Who's Who" of leaders in music and worship for the church in the mid-twentieth century. From left to right, this august body was composed of: Franklyn Weddle, Henry Livingston, Mable Carlile Hyde, Evan Fry, Harold Neal, secretary and pianist Norma Smith, Herbert Lively, Alice Edwards, Chris Hartshorn, Roy Cheville, Paul Craig, and Arthur Oakman.*

The KINGDOM of GOD on EARTH

Zion

431

Ether 5: 33
Ps. 43: 3
D. and C. 105: 5b

Roy A. Cheville

Lancashire 7.6.7.6.D.

M. ♩ 112

Henry Smart, 1813-1879

"Send Forth Thy Light, O Zion" as it first appeared in The Hymnal *of 1956*

Praise the Lord with trumpet sounding;
Let the voice him glorify;
Choir and instrument combining,
Of his goodness testify.

William Graves, *Hymns of the Saints,* number 53

X. Hymns of the Saints, 1981

DUE TO HEALTH CONCERNS, in 1969 Franklyn Weddle passed the baton (literally) to Harold Neal, who had been serving on the Graceland College music faculty. Neal's desire to continually upgrade the church's music resources led to the establishment in 1971 of the Committee on Congregational Music. The committee was composed of musicians, writers, and ministers from many varied backgrounds. Chaired by Harold Neal, the committee included Rosalee Elser, who arranged many of the musical settings, Barbara Higdon, Barbara Howard, Peter Judd, Aleta Runkle Page, Roger Revell, Ammon Roberson, Geoffrey Spencer, John Thumm, Alta Topham, Alan Tyree, Richard Clothier, and Kenneth Cooper, with assistance from John Obetz, Doris Harding Criss, and Carol Cavin.

There existed some feeling that, regardless of the statement in the preface of the 1956 hymnal, a number of the hymns in that collection *did* tend to be too "stilted and formal." In order to "test the waters" of opinion, the committee published two small supplements, in 1974 and 1976, respectively, with a total of twenty-five new hymns in various styles. The response was such that the Committee on Congregational Music soon became the new Hymnal Committee, and the result of their work, *Hymns of the Saints,* was published in 1981 (the same year, incidentally, that Harold Neal retired). The challenges felt by the committee were expressed in the preface to the work:

> The task of hymn selection has been a formidable one. The committee recognized that since the early 1960s organized religion, including our

> own church, has passed through a sort of crucible characterized by changing theological concepts, the searching eye of historical research, shifting modes of expression, and increased sensitivity to the sanctity of personhood. The committee was also very much aware that the range of musical taste in the church had widened considerably during the past two decades.[40]

The "wider range of musical taste in the church" prompted the inclusion in *Hymns of the Saints* of a variety of musical styles, including folk and lyrical-style melodic songs. These accompanied-melody songs, meant to be sung in unison, appear alongside the traditional hymn tunes in four-part chordal style that had inspired the long-standing RLDS tradition of robust part-singing. Even a few of the better old hymns and gospel songs from *Zion's Praises* and earlier collections were brought back, and several new hymns in the contemporary classical style were introduced, along with songs of diverse national origins.

The "increased sensitivity to the sanctity of personhood" referred to another challenge: the problem of inclusive language. The committee endeavored to implement the "Policy of Inclusive Language in Church Publications and Other Written Materials" adopted by the First Presidency in 1978, and, whenever possible, attempted to avoid gender-exclusive language (for example, the use of "men" to refer to "humankind"). As a result of this effort, to cite two examples, "Rise Up, O Men of God" became "Rise Up, O Saints of God," and in the Christmas hymn, "O Little Town of Bethlehem," the phrase "peace to men on earth" became "peace, good will on earth."

Other alterations were made in an effort to update archaic language or questionable theology. Thus, for example, in Parley Pratt's "Come, O Thou King of Kings," "all the chosen race" was altered to include "saints of every race." And the hymn "For All the Saints," was revised to include *living* Saints, and its antiquated imagery (such as "through gates of pearl streams in the countless host") updated (to the more expansive "from age to age resounds the countless host"). In the well-loved hymn "We Thank Thee, O God, for a Prophet," the assertion that "the wicked who fight against Zion will surely be smitten at last" was changed to the more positive declaration "The Saints who will labor for Zion will surely be blessed at last."

The high level of effort and care devoted to the selection and refinement of the hymns presented in this collection resulted in a rather lengthy period of time for its preparation. Often the work seemed to move forward with agonizing deliberateness. As those who have tried it know, it is not easy to make suitable alterations to well-known texts; just the right words or phrases have to be found that will enhance the message of a hymn, but not make it less poetic, less singable, or less distinguished.[41] In spite of challenges such as these, or perhaps because of them, the current hymnal has been exceptionally well accepted, and is certainly one of the most attractive and valuable hymnals yet produced by the church. And it is a tribute to the vitality of the organization that, the demanding standards set by the committee notwithstanding, about one in five of the texts and tunes in this collection of 501 hymns were either authored, composed, or arranged by church members past and present.

During the past fifteen years, the diversity of the church's musical repertoire has increased even more with the publication of three small supplemental hymnals. In 1994, in response to the emphasis on peace encouraged by President Wallace B. Smith, a collection of forty-six hymns on that topic was published under the title *Sing for Peace*. And in 1999, the church responded to requests from some of the membership to recognize the popular "contemporary Christian music" style by publishing *Sing a New Song*, a collection of fifty-two titles, including praise choruses and informal songs, twenty-three of them by church members. It could be argued that the role of this supplemental songbook was not unlike that of *Zion's Praises* of a century before, since both collections included some compositions that addressed a felt desire for songs that emphasized emotional appeal over thought and contemplation, and reflected to varying degrees the more popular style of their particular day.

The most recent supplement, *By Request*, was published in 2004 by the Worship Ministries department. It contains nineteen hymns, including newly composed works and requested favorites from recent World Conferences. Brief background statements for each song are included in the back of that collection.

Hymns from *Hymns of the Saints*, 1981

The Cause of Zion Summons Us

The desire to substantially upgrade the content of the hymns of the church resulted in the composition of a number of new texts for *Hymns of the Saints*, some of them by hymnal committee members themselves. One particular member of the group discovered a latent talent for the poetic expression of profound concepts. Geoffrey F. Spencer was able to articulate well many of the convictions and evolving doctrines of the church, as an example, the previously discussed concept of Zion.

Geoffrey Spencer spent the first thirty-eight years of his life in his native Australia, including his first twelve years as a church appointee. His parents encouraged the love he developed for music and singing, and the congregations he attended during those years gave him the opportunity to participate in choral music, both as a singer and sometimes as a conductor. As a high school teacher of English and an occasional director of school choirs, Spencer was able to indulge his love of the "word," and thereby develop a deep appreciation for the power of language, both written and sung.

Spencer served the church in many avenues and offices, culminating in ten years as a member of the Council of Twelve, four of these as its president. He has said that during these years, the part of his work he most enjoyed was visiting in the many congregations around the church and participating in their worship.

This particular text, "The Cause of Zion Summons Us," reflects a rather fresh understanding of Zion as a cause for which to labor rather than a finite goal to be completed, and proclaims, "Although fulfillment seems remote, the journey just begun, the Kingdom has already come, the victory is won." The text is set to the tune "St. Matthew," the work of the English composer William Croft.

Each of the hymns in this chapter are reproduced as they appear in *Hymns of the Saints*.

ZION AND THE KINGDOM

The Cause of Zion Summons Us 314

D. and C. 140:5c, d
D. and C. 137:6a

ST. MATTHEW C.M.D.
Alternate tune: ELLACOMBE (471)

Let Us Give Praise to the God of Creation

ANOTHER OF GEOFFREY SPENCER'S eleven hymns in *Hymns of the Saints* is notable for the efforts made by the author to capture in a few verses what he felt was the essence of Restoration theology. Spencer has explained how this hymn came into being:

> Frequently in my contacts in the field, I would encounter the question, in one form or another, "What does the church believe today?" What I attempted to do here was to incorporate into the text what I believed to be foundational beliefs of the Restoration. With this in mind, I referred briefly to the concepts of: (1) restoration; (2) the living presence of divine power for the task; (3) the sacredness of all things; (4) the unity of spirit and element; (5) the ongoing search for truth; (6) men and women together in ministry; (7) the role of the church as sin-bearer; (8) the power of our heritage; and (9) the experience of the God who calls us into the future. In the course of working up the text, I found other ideas pressing for inclusion, or so it seemed, but resisted the temptation to add other stanzas.[42]

These nine concepts were incorporated succinctly into the five stanzas of the hymn "Let Us Give Praise to the God of Creation." The tune, "Wesley," to which this unique text is sung was written by the nineteenth-century American musician and music educator Lowell Mason.

Geoffrey Spencer has left us an interesting glimpse into the way the hymn-writing process works best for him:

> My general method in developing a hymn text is strongly "perspirational." Rarely do I find lines coming easily and spontaneously. Most often I begin with a single notion, or germ idea, and let it rattle around in my mind. Phrases and terms tend to come at various intervals until I have the skeleton of a text. What follows after that is essentially hard work, dealing with rhyme, meter, freshness of language, and imagery.[43]

STEWARDSHIP

Let Us Give Praise to the God of Creation 398

D. and C. 137:6
D. and C. 140:5c, d

WESLEY 11.10.11.10.

Lord, in This Hour

WRITING WAS AN important part of Naomi Russell's life. She began to write poetry as a child, and this love of writing led to a rich career of forty-three years as assistant editor at Herald House, the church's publishing company. She has said that of the hundreds of works that have gone to press with her involvement, she believed that the words most frequently read have been those in *Hymns of the Saints.* Seven hymns in that collection were authored or coauthored by Naomi Russell.

Russell has shared a deeply personal testimony of the creation of this particular hymn, which begins, "Lord, in this hour enable us to see the breadth and depth of thine eternity." She explains, "I wrote this when we knew that our daughter would soon die of cancer. She had just finished getting her master's degree and was looking forward to teaching public school music when her affliction began. Three years later she passed away, leaving her husband and two young sons."[44]

Especially when seen in the context of their origin, the words of this hymn communicate a powerful testimony of the search for the perspective of the Eternal, where both life and death are seen as part of the natural flow of God's creation. "But life and light go on unendingly—one bright mosaic known alone to thee."

The tune, "Wiesbaden," has an interesting history as well. It was written by Dale Rider, an organist and composer living in Independence, Missouri. Dale and his wife Twyla are the persons who are largely responsible for the attractive appearance of *Hymns of the Saints.* In the summer of 1974, with the support of the church, they served an apprenticeship at the Henniger Music Studio in Wiesbaden, Germany. In addition to Dale's composing this tune while there, they both learned a painstaking but aesthetically pleasing method of music engraving, which was then used to produce the finished hymnal. Dale and Twyla currently serve as staff organists at the Auditorium and the Temple.

This insightful text can also be effectively sung to the familiar tune "Eventide," typically associated with "Abide with Me" (HS 128).

Lord, in This Hour

150

D. and C. 76:1, 2a, b
Romans 11:33, 34, 36

WIESBADEN 10.10.10.10.

The organ in the sanctuary of the Temple in Independence
(Photo by Val Brinkerhoff, courtesy Community of Christ)

Written in our history's pages
Are those times we've spent with you
When we've found your Spirit working
To transform our lives anew.
Barbara Howard, "God, Whose Grace Redeems Our Story"

XI. A New Hymnal for 2013

At this writing, a headquarters committee is at work on the selection process for hymns for a new Community of Christ hymnal, to be introduced at the World Conference of 2013. Preliminary plans are for it to contain approximately 750 songs in a variety of styles, including for the first time a significant number of indigenous songs of the various countries in which the church has a presence. New texts and tunes have been contributed by the membership, and a large number of fresh new hymns from other denominations have appeared during the now twenty-nine years since the publication of *Hymns of the Saints.*

The committee is made up of six persons at church headquarters: Jane Gardner, Peter Judd, Jan Kraybill, Bruce Lindgren, Joey Williams, and hymnal project administrator Lauren Hall. They have involved numerous additional people in evaluating newly submitted hymns, songs sent from the international field, and hymns from the current hymnals of other denominations. In addition, the membership at large was invited to respond by "voting" for their personal favorite hymns from *Hymns of the Saints* and the three supplements currently published by the church. It seems clear that the result of the committee's labor will be a hymnal for Community of Christ that will equal or surpass previous collections in the degree of diversity and variety that it will contain. And, it appears that it will be the largest hymnal the church has published in recent years, exceeded only by the hymnals of 1870 and 1889.

A Hymn for our Past, our Present, and our Future

God, Whose Grace Redeems Our Story

Although final decisions have not yet been made, one of the hymns on the 2013 hymnal committee's "short list" at press time is a hymn by Barbara Howard that carries a message that seems a particularly appropriate conclusion to this study of the heritage of the Reorganization.

Barbara and Richard Howard have served Community of Christ for many years. Both retired in 1995, Barbara as a Herald House editor and Richard as church historian. They have been collaborating on assignments since 1952, when they worked together on a Zion's League summer production of the play *The Green Pastures* in Independence, Missouri. They were married the following year. Both of the Howards have contributed eminently to church literature through numerous books and *Saints' Herald* articles, as well as through several hymns published in *Hymns of the Saints*, for which Barbara was a committee member.

"God, Whose Grace Redeems Our Story" is a prayer hymn that artfully affirms God's presence in our past (stanza one), our present (stanza two), and our hope for the future (stanza three). And, undergirding all the chapters of our lives is the fervent prayer that God's Spirit will continue to work within us "to transform our lives anew." It is a good hymn for an anniversary.

God, Whose Grace Redeems Our Story

Barbara Howard (1930-)

The Sacred Harp, 1844; arr. Rosalee Elser
BEACH SPRING

I will pray with the spirit
and I will pray with the mind also;
I will sing with the spirit
and I will sing with the mind also.

—I Corinthians 14:15 RSV

XII. Postlude: With Heart and Mind

These words of the apostle, addressing disorders in the worship of the church in Corinth, resound across the years to all who would seek to praise their Creator in song in their own day. His words affirm the importance of both fervor and substance in our worship, advice that may be of particular value to us today.

We have seen how, at times, some of the hymns from our past have seemed to emphasize emotion at the expense of thought, while others have tended to offer substance with little feeling. Paul is saying that we have been created in such a way that the proper balance of both heart and mind is vital to our worship as complete persons. In a word, worship and worship music should not only make us *feel,* but also make us *think.*

This vital balance may be increasingly difficult to achieve today in a culture that appears to value, even exalt, the pursuit of fleeting entertainment above nearly every other quest. At times, it appears that the line between worship and entertainment is becoming blurred, and we wonder just what we are really worshiping. Might it be an individual, a piece of music, a musical performance, or is it the Creator? Like all elements of Divine worship, music, *regardless of its type or style,* should not call undue attention to itself; it must be subordinate to the larger purpose it serves. When this fails to happen, it is possible for a congregation to worship or pay honor to the wrong thing—a song, or a musician, or even a particular speaker, rather than to God. Author and minister of music Marva Dawn calls this practice idolatry.[45] Her excellent book with the perceptive title *Reaching Out Without Dumbing Down,* discusses ways in which many churches have tried to "dumb down" their faith and their worship in a self-defeating, counter-productive effort to attract and maintain membership.

Thus, while both secular and sacred music are manifestations of the same art, the same Divine gift, there is one important difference. In secular music, it is permissible for the performers and the music itself to share the "spotlight," but in the practice of sacred music it is important for both to *get out of the way*, and allow the worshipers to focus on the Divine. A good musician or worship leader will strive to help the congregation see past themselves to the God who is the source of their gifts.

The sentimental style of music that was popular a century ago did not meet these criteria for genuine worship, and thus its use is now discouraged. Characteristics of that music often included a lack of creativity; a trite, repetitive, predictable quality in both its music and its words; a shallowness of theological and musical substance; and a distinct self-centeredness. These are still valid tests for the elements of worship today.

When Christ proclaimed that the true worshipers are those who will "worship the Father in spirit and in truth" (John 4:23), we were being assured that genuine worship involves both the heart and the head. Indeed, content without passion can be lifeless, while emotion without substance can be shallow. Neither passion nor substance alone is enough, but it is the proper nurture and balance of both that is so important to the development of whole persons, and to the true worship of their Creator.

* * *

As this brief exploration of our heritage of hymnody has illustrated, the catalogue of that which matters most in today's Community of Christ would differ in many ways from that of the early Reorganization. For example, we no longer insist on being the "one true church" with a monopoly on light and truth. We no longer preach the imminent second coming and Zionic reign of Christ, with the attendant destruction of non-believers. We no longer think of Zion as a specific place in Missouri to which the righteous can repair for safety in the "last days." We are learning to interpret certain events of our history in a more accurate light. Our hymns no longer seek to include a final stanza addressing life after death. We are learning to value diversity.

Throughout this evolution, however, our most important beliefs have not changed. To cite only a few examples, we continue to affirm the importance as well as the practice of the ongoing revelation of Divinity. We still rely on a well-prepared, self-sustaining ministry. We value the wisdom of the scriptures. And we enjoy a unique sense of community with members throughout the world.

Music can provide us with a good model of true community, and for discovering unity through our diversity. For, rather than everyone singing the same melody in unison, it can be much more satisfying to combine our many diverse yet agreeable melodies into a harmony that is much greater than the sum of its parts. In this way, our long heritage of part-singing in the Reorganization can be seen as a valid model for our goal of genuine community.

We have seen that our evolving beliefs can be traced through our heritage of hymns, accompanied by an evolution in musical styles. We appreciate to a greater extent the ability of gifted authors and composers to express and reveal the truths they perceived in their own time. If scripture is defined as the testimony of the revelation of Divinity to inspired men and women, then hymns may indeed be said to be a form of scripture and the hymnal a "fourth standard book." Like other scriptures, our hymns contain gems of wisdom, insight, and devotion, expressed more beautifully than we could express on our own. They are worthy of our study, our familiarity, and our whole-hearted enjoyment.

And so, with a greater appreciation of our past, we welcome the future. We await a new resource for worship and song, a new collection of hymns for the journey. The challenges facing us today certainly include the question of how best to deal with an ever more divergent range of models for music and worship, as we attempt to offer our faithful devotion to God. However this question is addressed, we know that the worship of the church must maintain its integrity, honor its heritage, and at the same time offer ministry to an increasingly diverse body of people throughout today's world. These are challenges that will be met joyfully as together we learn to discern the guidance of God's Holy Spirit for the way ahead.

Endnotes

[1] Roy A. Cheville, *They Sang of the Restoration* (Independence, MO: Herald Publishing House, 1955), 10. The book in which this phrase appears has been a valuable resource in the compilation of the present manuscript.

[2] Quoted in Carl Halter, *God and Man in Music* (St. Louis: Concordia Publishing House, 1963), 36–37.

[3] The total of nine hymnals for the Reorganization counts as a separate book the 1864 expanded version of Emma Smith's 1861 hymnal for the Reorganization.

[4] Community of Christ Doctrine and Covenants 24:3b. LDS Doctrine and Covenants 25:12.

[5] Linda King Newell and Valeen Tippetts Avery, *Mormon Enigma: Emma Hale Smith* (Garden City, NY: Doubleday, 1984), 12–13.

[6] B. H. Roberts, ed., *History of the Church of Jesus Christ of Latter-day Saints*, 2nd ed. rev. (Salt Lake City: Deseret Book, 1957), 1:270.

[7] Michael Hicks, *Mormonism and Music* (Urbana: University of Illinois Press, 1989), 20.

[8] Ibid.

[9] Hicks, 26–27.

[10] Hicks, 31.

[11] Roberts, 2:392.

[12] *Messenger and Advocate* 2, no. 18 (March 1836): 281.

[13] Zenos H. Gurley, writing in *The True Latter Day Saints' Herald* 1, no. 1 (January 1860): 18, and succeeding issues.

[14] Frederick B. Blair, comp., *The Memoirs of President W. W. Blair* (Lamoni, IA: Herald Publishing House, 1908), 16.

[15] *The True Latter Day Saints' Herald* 1, no. 10 (October 1860): 238.

[16] Ibid.

[17] Ibid., 244.

[18] Ibid.

[19] Hicks, 28–29.

[20] Ibid. It should be noted that Hicks's statement that "Redeemer of Israel" was absent from Emma's 1841 hymnal is inaccurate. It was simply omitted from the index.

[21] *The True Latter Day Saints' Herald* 1, no. 12 (December 1860): 292.

[21] *The True Latter Day Saints' Herald* 2, no. 5 (August 1861): 144. Emphasis in the original.

[23] Ruby C. Faunce, "Biography of Mark Hill Forscutt, arranged from his diaries," *The Saints' Herald* 81, no. 5 (January 30, 1934): 143.

[24] *History of the Reorganized Church of Jesus Christ of Latter Day Saints* (Independence, MO: Herald Publishing House, 1952), 3:519–520.

[25] *The Saints' Harp* (Lamoni, IA: Reorganized Church of Jesus Christ of Latter Day Saints, 1870), iv.

[26] Ibid., iv–v.

[27] *The History of the Reorganized Church of Jesus Christ of Latter Day Saints*, 3:629.

[28] Doctrine and Covenants 119 (Community of Christ version).

[29] The creative pseudonyms of this English-born Nebraska resident included "A. Nebraskan," "M. English," "A. Unicorn," "Fetteri," "Hilliare," "M.**," "Marcellus Ostracis,""Mareschal," and "Mu Phi."

[30] *The Saints' Harmony* (Lamoni, IA: Herald Publishing House, 1889), Preface.

[31] Ruby C. Faunce, "Biography of Mark Hill Forscutt, Arranged from His Diaries," *The Saints' Herald* 81 (July 31, 1934): 970. In *The Saints' Harmony*, Onderdonk's text was paired with the tune "Rathbun," while Forscutt's tune "Norman" was suggested for use with three other texts.

[32] Minutes of the 1895 General Conference of the Reorganized Church of Jesus Christ of Latter Day Saints, 25.

[33] *The Saints' Hymnal* (Independence, MO: Herald Publishing House, 1895), Preface.

[34] Another minor point of departure was that for the fifty hymns at the back without complete musical settings, the committee understandably found it necessary to include the entire first phrase of music rather than just an often-indistinguishable first measure.

[35] *Zion's Praises* (Lamoni, IA: Herald Publishing House, 1903), Introduction.

[36] Vida E. Smith, quoted in Carlyle F. Kueffer, ed., *Stories of Our Hymns* (Independence, MO: Herald Publishing House, 1938), 136. The "quarterly" refers to a Sunday School textbook of the day.

[37] Gordon Mesley, "Oral History Interviews with Franklyn S. Weddle (1972)," p. 11, Community of Christ Library-Archives, Independence, MO.

[38] *The Hymnal* (Independence, MO: Herald Publishing House, 1956), Preface, 7.

[39] *General Conference Bulletin*, October 8, 1958 (Independence, MO: Reorganized Church of Jesus Christ of Latter Day Saints), 87.

[40] *Hymns of the Saints* (Independence, MO: Herald Publishing House, 1981), Preface.

[41] In the case of hymns from other denominations, copyright holders would not always allow alterations, and a number of these were included without the changes that would have been preferred.

[42] Geoffrey Spencer, letter to the author, 1994.

[43] Ibid.

[44] Naomi Russell, letter to the author, 1994.

[45] Marva Dawn, *Reaching Out Without Dumbing Down* (Grand Rapids, MI: Wm. B. Eerdmans Publishing Co., 1995), 41 and following.

Appendix:
Major Hymnals of the Latter Day Saint Movement

(Not listed are several supplements, youth hymnals, unofficial hymnals, etc. Until 1889, hymnals were pocket-size and, except for Little and Gardner, contained words only.)

1835 *A Collection of Sacred Hymns, for the Church of the Latter Day Saints*. Kirtland. The first Emma Smith hymnal. Contained 90 hymns.

1840 *A Collection of Sacred Hymns, for the Church of the Latter Day Saints in Europe*. Manchester, England. Edited by apostles Pratt, Taylor, and Young. Used by LDS in Europe and America through 25 editions, until 1912.

1841 *A Collection of Sacred Hymns, for the Church of Jesus Christ of Latter Day Saints*. Nauvoo. Emma's second hymnal. Contained 304 hymns, including her original 90.

1844 *A Collection of Sacred Hymns for the Use of The Latter Day Saints*. Little and Gardner, Bellows Falls, VT (Unofficial). Contained 48 hymns, 31 with music.

1861 *The Latter Day Saints' Selection of Hymns*. Cincinnati. First RLDS hymnal, credited to Emma Smith and based on her 1841 Nauvoo hymnal. Contained 249 texts. Enlarged edition published in 1864.

1870 *The Saints' Harp*. Plano and Lamoni. Contained 1,120 hymns, 88 by Mark Forscutt.

1889 *Latter-day Saints' Psalmody*. Salt Lake City. Original LDS tunes for the texts in the Manchester Hymnal (see 1840).

1889 *The Saints' Harmony*. Lamoni. Split-page format, music on top, texts (all 1,120 texts from the *Saints' Harp*) on the bottom.

1895 *The Saints' Hymnal*. Lamoni. Replaced bulky *Saints' Harmony*. Contained 300 hymns with texts between the treble and bass clefs.

1903 *Zion's Praises*. Lamoni. Hymnal for the Sunday School movement, intended to be used along with *The Saints' Hymnal*.

1909 *Deseret Sunday School Songs*. Salt Lake City.

1927 *Latter-day Saint Hymns*. Salt Lake City. More traditional hymns, to be used along with *Deseret Sunday School Songs*.

1933 *The Saints' Hymnal*. Independence. Contained 442 hymns, including selections from both the 1895 *Saints' Hymnal* and *Zion's Praises*.

1948 *Hymns: Church of Jesus Christ of Latter-day Saints*. Salt Lake City. (Revised edition published in 1950.)

1956 *The Hymnal*. Independence. Contained 583 hymns. Increased attention to musical quality.

1981 *Hymns of the Saints*. Independence. Contains 501 hymns, wider variety of styles. Carefully edited for theological integrity, inclusive language.

1984 *Hymns of the Restoration*. Restoration Hymn Society, Independence. Contains 402 hymns.

1985 *Hymns of the Church of Jesus Christ of Latter-day Saints*. Salt Lake City. Contains 341 hymns. An extensive list of international translations available.

About the Author

RICHARD CLOTHIER is Professor Emeritus of music at Graceland University, Lamoni, Iowa. His responsibilities throughout the thirty-seven years of his Graceland career included teaching a wide range of music courses and, at various times, conducting the band, orchestra, directing the university's performing arts center, and serving as chair of the Division of Fine Arts. His service at Graceland was pleasantly interrupted for six years in the 1970s when he accepted the rare opportunity to head the music department and serve as an administrator at the American School in London, England.

A high priest in Community of Christ, Dick currently serves in the Lamoni Congregation, where he ministers in worship and music on a regular basis. Until moving to London, he was part of the committee that produced *Hymns of the Saints,* and has served in a consulting role for the upcoming 2013 hymnal. He is the author of numerous articles for various church periodicals, and his first book, *A Heritage of Hymns,* was published by Herald House in 1996.

Dick and his wife, Louita, also a well-known musician, have two adult children: Kathi Clothier Angeroth of Stanton, Nebraska; and David Clothier, currently working as a theatre lighting technician for Princess Cruise Lines.